TURNER CLASSIC MOVIES BRITISH FILM GUIDES

The Tauris British Film Guides series has since its launch in 2003 contributed to the revaluation of British cinema by going deep into key British films from the past hundred years. To carry the project forward, I.B.Tauris has now entered an exciting and innovative partnership with TCM (Turner Classic Movies), the premier movie channel dedicated to keeping the classic movies alive for fans old and new. With a striking new identity, the series will continue to provide what the *Guardian* has called a 'valuable resource of critical work on the UK's neglected film history'.

The series will continue to draw on all genres and all eras, building over time into a wide-ranging library of informed, in-depth film guides, demonstrating the variety, creativity, humanity, poetry and mythic power of the best of British cinema in volumes designed to be accessible to film enthusiasts, scholars and students alike.

TCM is the definitive classic movie channel available on cable, satellite and digital terrestrial TV <www.tcmonline.co.uk>

JEFFREY RICHARDS
General Editor

British Film Guides published and forthcoming:

TURNER CLASSIC MOVIE BRITISH FILM GUIDE

Black Narcissus

SARAH STREET

I.B. TAURIS
LONDON · NEW YORK

Published in 2005 by I.B.Tauris & Co Ltd
6 Salem Road, London W2 4BU
175 Fifth Avenue, New York NY 10010
www.ibtauris.com

In the United States of America and Canada distributed by Palgrave Macmillan
a division of St Martin's Press, 175 Fifth Avenue, New York NY 10010

ISBN 1 84511 046 3
EAN 978 1 84511 046 8

A full CIP record for this book is available from the British Library
A full CIP record for this book is available from the Library of Congress

Library of Congress catalog card: available

Set in Monotype Fournier and Univers Black by Ewan Smith, London
Printed and bound in Great Britain by MPG Books, Bodmin

Contents

Illustrations

Acknowledgements

My interest in *Black Narcissus* began when I was researching the reception of British films in the USA. The Margaret Herrick Library of the Academy Foundation, Los Angeles, was an essential source for material on the censorship of British films, and I thank archivist Barbara Hall for alerting me to the Legion of Decency material that proved to be so rich and fascinating. Sue Simkin accompanied me on that trip and shared with me the delights of archival research far away from home; I thank her for all the support she has given me throughout this project. I would also like to acknowledge the Popular European Cinema conference on 'The Spectacular', held at the University of Warwick in March 2000, for providing me with the opportunity to present my first conference paper on *Black Narcissus*, as well as other institutions that have invited me to speak about the film: Bath Spa University, the Institute of Historical Research, London (the *Issues in Film History* series), the University of the West of England, the University of Bristol Department of Drama: Theatre, Film, Television and the Colonialism Research Group conference at Bristol, 2004. Jeffrey Richards and Philippa Brewster were enthusiastic about the idea of publishing *Black Narcissus* in the British Film Guide series, and I thank them very much for providing me with the opportunity to bring my material together. I have loved working on a single film for a single book.

Several people were very helpful in assisting me to locate material as well as sharing their ideas with me: Priya Jaikumar, Duncan Petrie, Laurie Ede, Ian Christie and Judith Priestman. Sue Friedrich and Andrea Weiss corresponded with me about their films *Damned if You Don't* and *A Bit of Scarlet*, providing useful background information about their particular appropriations of *Black Narcissus*. Their films were particularly stimulating in demonstrating to me the film's longevity and ability to transcend the customary boundaries of national cinema and generic analysis.

The stills were obtained from the Bibliothèque du Film, Paris and the British Film Institute, London. The University of Bristol's Faculty of Arts Research Fund awarded financial assistance for the purchase of the illustrations. The cover still is reproduced courtesy of Carlton International Media Limited/Lfi. All stills are reproduced here for the purposes of critical analysis.

Film Credits

BLACK NARCISSUS

Production Company	The Archers/Independent Producers Ltd
Associate Producer	George R. Busby
UK Distributor	General Film Distributors
US Distributor	Universal
Director, Producer, Screenplay	Michael Powell and Emeric Pressburger Adapted from the novel by Rumer Godden
Assistant Director	Sydney Streeter
Music and Sound Score	Brian Easdale with the London Symphony Orchestra
Director of Photography	Jack Cardiff
Camera Operators	Ted Scaife, Chris Challis (uncredited)
Colour	Technicolor
Colour Control	Natalie Kalmus
Associate	Joan Bridge
Production Designer	Alfred Junge
Assistant Art Director	Arthur Lawson
Costumes	Hein Heckroth
Editor	Reginald Mills
Dubbing	Gordon K. McCallum
Sound	Stanley Lambourne, Western Electric Recording
Process Shots	Walter Percy Day
Running Time	101 minutes
UK Release	26 May 1947
US Release	13 August 1947

CAST

Deborah Kerr	Sister Clodagh
Sabu	The young General
David Farrar	Mr Dean
Flora Robson	Sister Philippa

Esmond Knight	The old General
Kathleen Byron	Sister Ruth
Jenny Laird	Sister Honey
Judith Furse	Sister Briony
May Hallatt	Angu Ayah
Shaun Noble	Con
Eddie Whaley Jr	Joseph Anthony
Nancy Roberts	Mother Dorothea
Jean Simmons	Kanchi
Ley On	Phuba (Mr Dean's servant)

ONE
Origins

I wandered away from the others and going down a steep little path came upon a grave; it was marked only by a small headstone in the shape of a cross with a name, 'Sister ... ' and two dates; she had died when she was only twenty-three.

No one could tell me anything about her; no other graves were near, no sign of any mission, but the villagers had made her grave a shrine; it was daubed with whitewash and there were offerings: a saucer of rice, an egg – in India eggs are thought particularly valuable – a string of marigolds.

I never saw that grave again, for all I know it may have disappeared but, twelve years later in that bunk on board the *Orion* I began: 'The Sisters left Darjeeling in the last week in October. They had come to settle in the General's palace at Mopu which was now to be known as the Convent of St Faith ... '[1]

This memory, as Rumer Godden recalls in her autobiography, was the genesis of her first best-selling novel, *Black Narcissus* (1939), completed as she was returning from India to England just before giving birth to her second daughter in 1938. Godden had already written two novels, *Chinese Puzzle* (1936) and *The Lady and the Unicorn* (1937), but it was *Black Narcissus* that brought her literary and financial success, a novel that remains perhaps her best-known work. It drew on her experience of India where she had spent a good deal of her childhood and where she lived with her children during the Second World War. Godden was born in Eastbourne, Sussex, in 1907 and was taken to India by her parents when she was six months old. Her father, Arthur Leigh Godden, was a steamer agent stationed in India. In 1913 Rumer and her sister Jon were sent to England to live with their paternal grand-mother and their aunt, returning to India on the outbreak of the First World War and then to school in England in 1920. The experience of living in two places and of being exposed to two cultures was highly influential in Godden's prolific literary output, which by the end of her career consisted of many novels, short stories, non-fiction works and children's literature.

Black Narcissus clearly draws on Godden's personal connections with India, experience of displaced living and fascination with cross-cultural exchange. The novel is about an order of Anglo-Catholic nuns with their headquarters in Canstead, Sussex, who establish a school and dispensary in Mopu, a deserted palace in the hills north of Darjeeling built by General Ranajit Rai on land leased from the Government of India. He used the palace as a harem, 'The House of Women', but after his death his son, General Toda Rai, turned out the women and invited a Christian group, 'The Brothers of St Peter' to open a school in the palace in an attempt to expunge the 'impression of evil' he felt was lingering there.[2] The Brothers, however, left after five months because they felt they were not needed, that their work would be better carried out elsewhere. Toda Rai then offered the premises to the nuns in another attempt to do good on his estate, seeing himself as an enlightened ruler.

The mission is led by Sister Clodagh, a relatively young nun to be given such a responsibility. She is accompanied by several other nuns, in particular Sister Ruth, an 'uncomfortable person ... young and oddly noticeable', who finds it hard to settle in the new environment, as does Clodagh, who is reminded of her former life before she joined the Order, in particular of a failed love affair in Ireland.[3] Mr Dean, the General's English agent, assists the nuns when they arrive at Mopu but is sceptical about their chances of making a success of their venture, an opinion shared by Angu Ayah, a woman who has been the caretaker of the palace for many years. Sister Clodagh relies on Mr Dean for practical assistance in the conversion of the palace, but she is uncomfortable about doing this since she has been warned that he has 'gone native; lives like one and they say he drinks and is ... bad with women'.[4] Another problem is the continuing evidence of Sister Ruth's disturbance: 'When she was angry nowadays, she could not help what she did or what she said, because she did not know. It felt like something dark and wet, flooding into her brain, like blood.'[5]

The nuns are forced to make compromises as they adapt to their new environment. Since they need an interpreter, they take in a young local boy, Joseph Anthony, and Sister Clodagh agrees to allow the General's heir, Dilip Rai (the young General) to attend the school, even though he turns out to be a distracting presence, handsome and dressed in fine costumes: 'He was outside everything they had considered real; he was the impossible made possible.'[6] In particular, he reminds Clodagh of her past love, Con, and leads her into daydreaming instead of praying or getting on with her duties. As Godden explains, 'Clodagh herself was sometimes curiously absent-minded as she read the prayers; occasionally she said a prayer through twice, and once, at the end of Compline, she kept them keeling there for nearly ten minutes.'[7] Against her better judgement Mr Dean persuades Clodagh to take in Kanchi, a local orphan girl, who becomes another unsettling intrusion, since she 'was like a basket of fruit, thought Clodagh, piled high and luscious and ready to eat. Though she looked shyly down, there was something steady and unabashed about her; the fruit was there to be eaten, she did not mean to let it rot.'[8] Combined with the vibrant locale and constant wind blowing through the palace, these characters prevent the nuns from concentrating on their mission, frustrating the plans they had clearly laid out for the school and dispensary.

The novel provides many examples of the nuns feeling unsettled. Sister Philippa, who works in the garden, is so distracted that she plants flowers instead of vegetables and asks to be transferred to another convent; Ruth becomes increasingly unstable and difficult to manage. She is infatuated with Mr Dean and jealous of Clodagh's contact with him. When Sister Adela, a nun from a convent in Canton, joins them she is shocked to see how far the nuns have lapsed from their duties and dismayed by their dependence on Mr Dean. Their problems escalate when the young General runs off with Kanchi and a sick baby dies. One of the nuns gives its mother some lotion even though Sister Briony, the sister in charge of the dispensary, has advised against treatment after taking heed of Mr Dean's warning that treating very serious cases runs the risk of being ostracised by the local community if the patient subsequently dies. After the death of the baby none of the local people returns to the school or dispensary.

Ruth escapes from the convent in search of Mr Dean and declares her love for him. Seeing that she is extremely agitated, he offers to take her back to the convent. She insists that she will return alone and leaves. Mr Dean does not report Ruth's visit to Clodagh immediately because he has been drinking; back at the convent the nuns are frantic with worry about her. As Clodagh waits for news she senses that someone is watching her. She goes out to ring the bell:

A wet hand came over her shoulder, and an arm with a mad strength.

The bell jerked with a clang. Her fingers tore at Sister Ruth's arms and her gripping hands, that were pushing and forcing her to the railings. She hung over them, balanced on the wet block, swaying above the gulf. Then her boot slipped on the stone and she fell heavily sideways, missing the railings and hitting the gravel beside the block.

As she fell she snatched at Sister Ruth.

She had a vision of her mad wet face against the sky, as she rocked on to the slippery stone. She tried to catch at her habit to help her, but the stuff was slimy with wet and dirt. Then Sister Ruth seemed to fall into the sky with a scream, as she went over the railings.[9]

After Sister Ruth's death the nuns decide to leave Mopu. Sister Clodagh writes to Mother Dorothea, the Mother Superior who had originally charged her with leading the mission of St Faith, telling her of their failure. Out of the tragedy, however, the novel ends with Clodagh developing a new sense of spiritual renewal. Even though Mr Dean's prediction that the convent would not be a success has been proved correct, she leaves with a greater understanding of herself and her spiritual purpose, telling Mr Dean that she will be sent to another convent. As an appropriate closure to their momentous experiences, the rains break as they leave Mopu.

Published in January 1939, *Black Narcissus* was a critical and popular success in Britain, Europe and America. Its well-crafted story of exotic disturbance and forbidden passion gripped readers and Godden was declared to be an exciting new novelist.[10] She writes in her autobiography that she was unaware of the publication date and was taken by surprise when she saw a banner announcing the novel's title and her name while travelling by bus along Charing Cross Road, London.[11] Its success gave her confidence in her writing abilities and she immediately started work on another project, the novel *Gypsy Gypsy*, as well as short stories. The immense popularity of *Black Narcissus* was instrumental in Powell and Pressburger's decision to adapt it for the screen, since on different occasions they were both introduced to it by enthusiastic women readers. By the time they were planning the film in 1946 both the novel and its author had acquired a prestigious and popular reputation.

POLITICAL AND GENERIC CONTEXTS

The subject matter of *Black Narcissus* was intimately connected to its immediate political context. In 1939 India was heading towards independence from British rule (achieved in 1947, the date of the Indian Independence Act) and Godden's story of the difficulties that faced the nuns, leading to the abandonment of their mission, can be read as a narrative about the decline of empire and failure of imperialism. The timing of the film's release in Britain (May 1947) coincided with increasing communal violence in India as protracted disputes continued over the form of government that should be established on the dissolution of the British Empire. The Indian Independence Act was hurried through in July in an attempt to quell the violence. It created two new dominions, a predominantly Hindu India and a predominantly Muslim Pakistan, a controversial solution that led to many subsequent conflicts. Both the novel and the film therefore provide an interesting Western cultural reflection on the volatile political situation in India. Rumer Godden's life in India was not that of the typical Englishwoman. While she did not commit herself openly to support Indian nationalism, she was associated with unconventional behaviour. In 1928, for example, she established the Peggie Godden School of Dance, which took English, Indian and Eurasian pupils, to the chagrin of the English social elite in Calcutta. When she started a chorus dancing class for older Eurasian girls she received an offensive anonymous letter; gossip abounded that her school was less than respectable and that she was part-Indian herself.[12]

Godden's biographer has commented that *Black Narcissus* is about 'why the British had to leave India, and why much of what they had tried to do there was bound to fail'.[13] As a novel it therefore bears comparison with other decline-of-empire texts, including E. M. Forster's *A Passage to India* (1924) and Paul Scott's 'Raj Quartet' novels (1966–75). These novels fall into the tradition of what Edward Said has generally termed 'Orientalism', or the cultural construction of the East as Other – a world Western travellers encounter, but 'we are left at the end with a sense of the pathetic distance still separating "us" from an Orient destined to bear its foreignness as a mark of its permanent estrangement from the West'.[14] Godden's work is inflected with this sensibility, even though, as we shall see, the film, with its distinctive, powerful evocation of place, is perhaps more complicated in its representation of East–West relations. As a British author who spent many years of her life in India, Godden was drawn to imperial themes, most notably in *Black Narcissus* and *The River* (1946), a novel also set in India, later filmed by Jean Renoir. While the film versions of Godden's novels explored place in ways that were distinctive, it

was the source novels' actute awareness of space and place – the relation between the palace at Mopu and its immediate environs in *Black
Narcissus* and *The River*'s narrative set within the limits of a garden
– that provided Powell, Pressburger and Renoir with opportunities to
visualise 'the East' in striking cinematic terms.

As well as drawing on a literary source, Powell and Pressburger
were also working within an established popular genre of British and
Hollywood empire films that had proved to be successful at the British
box-office during the 1930s.[15] In general terms, the films focused on
the male experience of empire, usually from an upper-class imperialist
perspective. The 'white man's burden' was to maintain order and incul-
cate obedience in the colonies. As well as articulating this ideological
imperative, the empire genre seduced British and American audiences
by exploiting elements of spectacular epic cinema: lavish colour, exotic
landscapes, large casts, horses, regalia, military trappings, dances and
costumes. Several of the British films were produced by Alexander
Korda and directed by his brother, Zoltan (particularly *Elephant Boy*,
1937, *The Drum*, 1938 and *The Four Feathers*, 1939), while key American
examples of the genre are *The Lives of a Bengal Lancer* (1935), *The
Charge of the Light Brigade* (1936) and *Gunga Din* (1939). As Prem
Chowdhry has pointed out, these 'classic' Western representations of
empire offered a generally dichotomous relationship between white
colonialists and 'unruly natives' in their narratives about conquerors
and the conquered, civilisation and wilderness, and with an emphasis
on masculinity, action and bravery.[16] The genre has been compared to
the American western, as observed by Marcia Landy:

> If the western deployed the popular mythology of westward expansion-
> ism, the colonization of the American Indian, and the appropriation of
> the frontier couched in religious and nationalist terms (America as the
> New Eden and the Virgin land), the empire film translated expansion-
> ism, colonization, and commerce into a spectacle of benevolence of
> high-minded heroes acting in the name of royal prerogatives, culture
> against anarchy, and the white man's burden.[17]

Although the films glorify the imperial mission, as I have argued elsewhere, the contradictions of colonialism were beginning to surface in
films such as *The Drum*: 'On the one hand we are presented with a
picture of tolerance and benign British interest in India, while on the
other unspoken prejudices and racial tensions are clearly evident.'[18]

There was a pronounced gender aspect to these representations, as

Ella Shohat and Robert Stam observe: 'In many colonial films, colonial women become the instrument of the White male vision, and are granted a gaze more powerful than that of non-Western women and men.'[19] As nationalist movements gained ground and as pressure for Indian independence was increasing in the 1940s, cinematic representations of empire tended to offer more complex and ambivalent positions on questions of imperial rule, not least to prevent controversial reception in colonial territories. Chowdhry's analysis of *The Rains Came* (1940), for example, shows how certain stereotypes were altered to include aspects of native collusion and that there was a perceptible shift in the gender balance of imperial representation towards the feminine. This was significant because 'the substitution of the white female in place of the white male as the imperial protagonist had a range of ideological consequences, such as adding to the essence of "whiteness". The emphasis on the non-threatening woman and therefore feminine nature of imperialism opened up possibilities for negotiating a different agenda within the colonial setting.'[20]

Black Narcissus concentrates on female characters' experience of the East and can therefore be related to this changing focus of imperial representation that questioned many of the stock characters and Western certainties to be found in the empire films of the 1930s. At the same time this shift in emphasis operated as an ideological containing structure for many of the contradictions that were surfacing within the imperial mission. Deflecting questions of colonial and quasi-colonial rule on to feminine experience was, as Richard Dyer has pointed out, a striking feature of end-of-empire fictions, since 'when a text is one of celebration, it is the manly white qualities of expansiveness, enterprise, courage and control (of self and others) that are in the foreground; but when doubt and uncertainty creep in, women begin to take centre stage. The white male spirit achieves and maintains empire; the white female soul is associated with its demise.'[21] As we shall see, the range of such articulations in *Black Narcissus* renders it an extremely appropriate cultural expression of the end of British rule in India: not only are the central characters female, they are also nuns whose souls are literally in crisis.

POWELL, PRESSBURGER AND *BLACK NARCISSUS*

The films of Michael Powell and Emeric Pressburger constitute a distinctive corpus in the history of British cinema. Their partnership began in

1939 when both were working for Alexander Korda at Denham Studios on *The Spy in Black*, an espionage thriller. Powell had already gained experience directing films for Gaumont-British, while Pressburger, a Hungarian émigré who had come to Britain in 1933, had written screenplays in France and Germany. They went on to collaborate for eighteen years, forming The Archers company in 1943, for which they made their most celebrated films.

Powell and Pressburger's films acquired a reputation for being experimental during the Second World War, when they combined propaganda with spectacle. *The Lion Has Wings* (1939) and *One of Our Aircraft is Missing* (1941), in particular, were admired for their contribution to the war effort. *The Life and Death of Colonel Blimp* (1943), a film which drew on the buffoonish cartoon character created by Sidney Low, was, however, controversial for its satirical portrayal of the military, and was criticised by both Winston Churchill and the Ministry of Information. While several critics admired their films, they were on the whole regarded as being at odds with the prevailing style of British cinema, which was more wedded to the codes of realism. Although it is important not to exaggerate the extent to which they eschewed realism, they were drawn to subject-matter that involved fantasy and illusion. This was demonstrated particularly in their spectacular experiment with time and colour in *A Matter of Life and Death* (1946), a film in which David Niven stars as a pilot on the verge of death. In collaboration with set designer Alfred Junge, who also worked with them on *Black Narcissus*, Powell and Pressburger created an imaginative and innovative representation of heaven (in black-and-white; colour for earth) for scenes in which the pilot has to present a case to allow him to remain on earth to marry an American woman with whom he has just fallen in love. They also worked extremely well with cinematographer Jack Cardiff on this film, consolidating his experiments with Technicolor, which featured in many subsequent collaborations, including *Black Narcissus*.

Black Narcissus would not, on first examination, appear to be obvious material for a film by Powell and Pressburger, although its overall theme of confronting the nature of the world can be related to their earlier films.[22] While they had established a reputation for bold, experimental film-making their films seldom privileged female experience, with perhaps the exception of *I Know Where I'm Going!* (1945). This film is about a young woman who journeys from Manchester to Scotland, where she discovers that her destiny is far from what has been dictated by her background or experience. As Joan Webster (Wendy Hillier) is on course to be married to a rich industrialist she is forced to question her identity, beliefs and values when she finds herself attracted instead to a Scottish laird, swept away by a magical, mythical world she encounters in the Scottish highlands.[23] The film's title thus suggests a profound irony about being too confident about knowing the future: the more one is set on a certain course the less one is able to cope with sudden change, even though it may in the end be beneficial. Similarly, Godden's novel focuses on the nuns' experience of having their chosen path disrupted. In the old palace at Mopu they are prey to distractions and desires that have been unleashed by the overwhelming sense of place, the seductiveness of the East and the haunting resonance of their private memories. Firmly held beliefs are challenged, as they are forced to confront the instabilities of identity and of the imperial mission.

It is not surprising that on different occasions women introduced Powell and Pressburger to the best-selling novel. Powell recalls that during the Second World War the actress, Mary Morris, who had worked with him on *The Spy in Black* (1939) and *The Thief of Bagdad* (1940), recommended *Black Narcissus* for adaptation and that she was keen on playing the part of Sister Ruth.[24] As the novel demonstrates, Ruth's character is compelling and of central importance: her death is a cathartic event and it is her grave that relates to Godden's recollection from the past that acted as a creative trigger when she wrote the novel. While Morris was unsuccessful in persuading Powell to cast her in the film (the part of Sister Ruth was eventually played by Kathleen Byron), he was convinced that the novel would make a wonderful film: 'I could see that the story, so coolly told in excellent prose, would be wildly exotic and erotic on screen.'[25]

Pressburger's wife Wendy introduced him to the novel, which he optioned in 1945 after meeting Rumer Godden. Most of Pressburger's previous screenplays had been original, but this was an adaptation, a step he was somewhat sceptical about taking, since in his view: 'It is certainly very, very difficult to take a book and suddenly subjugate your own talent, which cannot be exactly the same as the talent of the writer of this book has been, so it will be a compromise, it must be a compromise.'[26] Godden had adapted the novel for a play produced by Lee Strasberg in 1942 in the USA, but allowed Pressburger to handle the screen adaptation, believing that he would 'treat *Black Narcissus* right if he ever gets it past the censor'.[27] Judging from *Variety*'s review of the play when it was performed in Maplewood, New Jersey, Godden's adaptation was not a success, the reviewer commenting that it needed 'judicious pruning and much sharper character delineation. In its present form the play is rambling and its two-dimensional characters, more often than not, are tripped up on their own verbosity.'[28] It was perhaps this experience that persuaded Godden to allow Powell and Pressburger to develop a screenplay which kept fairly close to the novel in terms of structure and intent but differed in several significant ways, which will be examined when the two are compared. Godden's objections to the film seemed to lie less with the adaptation and more with Powell's visualisation of the East, which she considered inauthentic. When she took her parents to the première she agreed with her father's criticism that much of it was inaccurate since none of it had been filmed in India. Her father referred to the costumes worn by the General and young General as 'pantomime clothes' – far more elaborate than what would have normally been worn.[29] As Chrisholm observes: 'Rumer came to feel that the film, although it stayed relatively close to her story, was not true to her intentions, and she would always react irritably when it was praised for its many admirable qualities.'[30] This bitterness was intensified when she later complained that Powell and Pressburger had persuaded her to part with the film rights to her novel for too low a figure: £1,800 with no percentage, apparently on the grounds that The Archers was a struggling company.[31]

PRE-PRODUCTION

Once Powell and Pressburger had decided to produce a film of *Black Narcissus* their first challenge was to convey the powerful sense of place that is so significant a factor in distracting the nuns from their 'civilising' mission. While Powell is often credited for his love of location shooting, he was at this time fascinated by what could be achieved in a studio. He was a supporter of what became known as the 'independent frame', a production method of concentrating as much activity in a studio as possible, with an emphasis on pre-planning and use of special effects. The aim was to cut costs and rationalise production, but also to create an environment in which technicians could experiment as a creative team.[32] *Black Narcissus* provided Powell with a perfect text with which to experiment with studio techniques, since it was decided that location shooting in India was impractical, as Powell noted in his autobiography:

The atmosphere in this film is everything, and we must create and control it from the start. Wind, the altitude, the beauty of the setting – it must all be under our control. If we went to India and shot a lot of exteriors, according to the usual plan, and then came back to Pinewood and then tried to match them here, you would have two kinds of colour and two kinds of style.[33]

The production ended up being a combination of Pinewood sets and some location shooting in a famous sub-tropical garden at Leonardslee in Horsham, Surrey, owned by Sir Giles Loder. The gardens, open to the public today and resplendent with azaleas and rhododendrons, are located in a 240-acre valley with seven lakes. Powell persuaded his initially sceptical production team that this was by far the best way forward:

I reminded them how British merchant princes and pro-consuls when they retired and come back to Britain to live, would bring whole trees and bushes wrapped in matting to remind them of India. Himalayan plants and trees do well in the British climate. Rhododendrons and azaleas grow like weeds. Leonardslee had a deep and steep little glen planted with cedars and deodars. You would swear you were in the Himalayas.[34]

The result was a highly controlled sense of place in keeping with Powell and Pressburger's conviction that, above all, this aspect of the production had to be perfect. As Kevin Macdonald has observed: 'Not for a moment are we allowed to escape this deliberate world of saturated Technicolor pigments, spectacular precipices and precarious buildings.'[35] It is somewhat ironic that the pre-determined, artificial creation of the film's diegetic world gave the impression of being wild, disturbing and natural. The decision to use Technicolor was a highly significant aspect of Powell and Pressburger's vision for the 'look' of the film. They had experimented with Technicolor on several occasions, most notably in *The Thief of Bagdad*, *The Life and Death of Colonel Blimp* and *A Matter of Life and Death*. As we shall see in the detailed analysis of *Black Narcissus*, its use in enhancing the film's expressionism is striking. The studio environment facilitated a stylisation of the East that was remarkable for its refusal of the documentary conventions undoubtedly favoured by Godden. Powell later boasted of how many people were convinced that he had filmed on location in India, a claim that contradicts Godden's adverse reaction to the authenticity of the sets.[36] Undoubtedly they conveyed a sense of verisimilitude that was convincing on a cultural level. Although the film's pressbook claimed that extensive research had been undertaken into the area, its people, their customs and costumes, there is no doubt that Powell and his technical team produced a vision of the East that originated very much in the Western imagination.

TECHNICAL TEAM

The level of control envisaged by Powell necessitated a team of expert technicians capable of delivering a spectacular vision of the East. Of key importance was cinematographer Jack Cardiff, who had been chosen by Technicolor when he was working at Denham Studios to experiment with the process first introduced to the UK in 1936. Although he did not have the advanced technical knowledge possessed by his colleagues, Cardiff persuaded Technicolor that he would be the best technician to develop the system because of his knowledge of painting. In his interview he impressed the representatives from Technicolor by citing examples of striking uses of light in the paintings of Vermeer and Rembrandt.[37] Cardiff had previously worked for Powell on *The Life and Death of Colonel Blimp* (as camera operator) and on *A Matter of Life and Death* (as photographer). As Duncan Petrie has pointed out, Cardiff worked towards developing a subtle use of Technicolor, using coloured light and filters while maintaining an expressionistic feel more commonly associated with black-and-white cinematography.[38] Martin Scorsese later referred to this as representative of the 'British school' of Technicolor that differed from its more typical deployment in brasher, garish Hollywood musicals or big outdoor pictures.[39] While the use of colour will be discussed in more detail later, Cardiff's contribution to the 'look' of the film must be noted from the outset as a crucial element in the seductive evocation of place, for which he won an Academy Award. While Rumer Godden was generally critical of the film, she noted in her autobiography that the cinematography 'almost magically' redeemed the film since 'he even managed to get a sense of the altitude'.[40]

Other notable members of the technical team included camera operators Chris Challis and Ted Scaife. Challis had also been involved in the development of Technicolor in Britain in the late 1930s, and during the Second World War he served as a cameraman in the RAF. He collaborated with Jack Cardiff on several occasions and the training he received on *Black Narcissus* enabled him to progress to the role

1. *The set at Pinewood showing that the bell is in fact only a few feet off the ground.*

2. *Alfred Junge's drawing of a nun ringing the bell.*

3. *Alfred Junge's drawing of a nun at bell viewed from behind and showing precipice.*

4. *Alfred Junge's drawing of the palace high on top of the hills.*

of cinematographer on The Archers' next film, *The End of the River* (1947).[41] Ted Scaife had worked for Technicolor since 1940, and was camera operator on several key films of the 1940s including *The Life and Death of Colonel Blimp*, *Caesar and Cleopatra* (1945), *Black Narcissus* and *The Third Man* (1949). Also of key importance to the creative team on *Black Narcissus* were art director Alfred Junge and associate art director (costumes) Hein Heckroth.

Junge was a German production designer in the early–mid 1920s working for Ufa in Berlin, before he moved to Britain. He worked extensively throughout the 1930s for Gaumont-British and then for MGM's British productions. During this period he produced some of the most distinctive designs in British cinema, creating, for example, the art deco sets for Jessie Matthews's musicals. His work was heavily influenced by his background in theatre, transferring a distinctive stylistic sensibility to cinema with the objective of 'convey[ing] both atmosphere and meaning through an overriding design concept, encompassing every visual aspect'.[42] He first designed for Powell on *The Fire Raisers* (1933), and in subsequent years created the sets for *Contraband* (1940), *The Life and Death of Colonel Blimp*, *A Canterbury Tale* (1944), *I Know Where I'm Going!* and *A Matter of Life and Death*.[43] His most celebrated sets for this film are the grand staircase and celestial court in heaven. Pinewood and Leonardslee gardens gave him ample scope to devise ingenious set designs that demonstrate the full technical achievement represented by *Black Narcissus*. Location photographs reveal how the bell tower was actually only a few feet above the ground. Junge's drawings and their realisation in the finished film however create the impression that the Convent of St Faith is located high in the mountains, on a terrifying precipice from which Sister Ruth falls so dramatically to her death. Powell greatly appreciated Junge's abilities as a 'gifted sketch artist' in helping him to visualise such scenes.[44] (See illustrations 1–3 of a nun at the bell tower). Junge's drawing shows the precise visualisation of the shot and the still reveals the constructed set just a few feet above ground. Even though he was involved in films that often required fantastical sets, Junge was described by Powell as very much a realist in terms of getting details precise and correct for each set. Thus, his celebrated models for *Black Narcissus* were constructed very precisely, as were the sketches that indicated the dimensions of the palace (see illustration 4). Powell later described Junge as 'the greatest art director that films have ever known ... I have never known anyone to touch him, to come near him'.[45] His esteemed reputation enabled him to command a key role in the production process. As an indication of how important Junge's designs were to the film, the total budget for sets was £78,176, whereas the actors cost a total of £50,465.[46]

Heckroth was a surrealist painter who also worked as a production and costume designer in German theatre. The Jooss Ballet employed him as an art director before he emigrated to Britain in 1935 with the ballet company and his Jewish wife Ada. For a few years Heckroth worked in the London theatre and also taught at Dartington Hall. He designed sets for Kurt Weill and Brecht's *A Kingdom for a Cow* at the Savoy Theatre, London, a production that did not run because of the start of the Second World War. During the early years of the war he was interned and sent to Australia, but was later allowed to return to take up the work at Denham Studios he had obtained through his theatrical contacts.[47] He did not work on films until towards the end of the war, when he designed costumes for *Caesar and Cleopatra* (1945) and *A Matter of Life and Death*. The costumes for the latter were particularly striking, the film's imaginative premise giving Heckroth full rein to experiment with both contemporary and historical costumes. Even though Heckroth's key input into Powell and Pressburger's films was not really prominent until *The Red Shoes* (1948), the costumes he designed for *Black Narcissus* were a notable adjunct to Cardiff's cinematography and Junge's sets.

The film's pressbook makes much of the costumes and how they were made largely from fabrics and drapes that were produced in the UK for export only. Permission was apparently given by the Board of Trade to use exotic prints and fabrics in this way.[48] Heckroth is reported as having conducted extensive research in libraries, magazines and by interviewing travellers who knew the Himalayas well. The Archers had a 'liaison officer' in India who sent back samples of original clothing, fur coats, hats, boots, jewellery and other materials which Heckroth used as a basis for his designs, which were 'based on authentic native clothes, but including a dash of imagination and bearing in mind the colour combinations that can be used with Technicolor'.[49] Rumer Godden generally thought that the majority of the costumes were too elaborate, describing them as 'pantomime clothes' and noting that in reality 'A rajah or Maharajah only wore such things for a durbar, a wedding or a state ball; their usual dress was a dark cloth achkan, or long coat, buttoned up to a high collar and with it fine white pantaloons cut like jodhpurs.'[50] This interesting divergence points to Heckroth's decision to make the costumes stand out with a deliberate, heightened exoticism in keeping with the creation of the East as 'Other'. While extensive research was undertaken for the costumes, 'authentic' designs were therefore appropriated to meet the particular demands of the film. The nuns' habits were a sort of oatmeal colour – deliberately so to create a contrast with the other colours used for the 'Eastern' environment and also with the vibrancy of the flashbacks in Ireland. As Herb Lightman observed:

> The sharp difference in psychology between the natives and nuns is symbolized in the contrast between their respective habits. The brightly coloured costumes of the natives blend naturally with the flamboyant chambers of the palace, but contrast sharply with the austere white vestments of the nuns. The local Indian ruler and his son appear in lavishly bejeweled costumes of gold brocade and sequins – creating a private blaze of color wherever they go.[51]

Heckroth's preparatory drawings and sketches for the costumes detail the variations of the elaborate attire worn by Dilip Rai (the young General). They also show the development of the design for the nuns' habits and wimples. These are striking in that they appear to envelop the head in a flowing movement while at the same time serve as a frame for the face.[52]

The artificially created world required for *Black Narcissus* also called on the skills of matte painters Walter Percy ('Poppa') Day and his sons, since many of the 'locations' were scenes painted on glass. Day, described by Powell as 'the greatest trick-man and film wizard that I've ever known', was a special effects director who had trained as a photographer and also studied at the Royal Academy of Art, London.[53] In 1919 he worked for a British company, Ideal Films, before moving to France, where he worked during the 1920s and then returned to Britain in the 1930s. His main employment there was with London Film Productions on a range of distinguished films including *The Private Life of Henry VIII* (1933) and *Things to Come* (1936). In the 1940s he worked for Powell and Pressburger on several occasions, directing the effects on *A Canterbury Tale*, devising the famous 'whirlpool sequence' in *I Know Where I'm Going!* and also creating memorable effects such as the moving staircase/escalator in *A Matter of Life and Death*, the film that was so influential as a precursor for the technical experimentation of *Black Narcissus*. Day is credited with developing many early special effects, including use of glass shots and matte painting. Jack Cardiff explained how these effects were employed on *Black Narcissus*.

5. *Illustration of the matte technique as used in Black Narcissus.*

very clear day — big, white peak

6. *Alfred Junge's drawing of the same setting, showing the basis for the eventual matte painting*

He recalled how they 'would matte out the "NG" parts of the frame with black card very exactly and then rephotograph the painted glass with mountains and clouds as a second exposure of the film'.[54] These techniques made it possible to work with the challenging demands of lighting for Technicolor stock since glass shots and matte painting facilitated the manufacture of exteriors in the studio where light conditions could be more highly controlled than on location. Illustrations 5 and 6 show the preparation for a typical scene, revealing the blacked-out matte area of the shot and then Alfred Junge's drawing under which he has written, 'very clear day – big, white peak', to describe the detail for the matte painting.

Much in the same spirit of ingenious creativity that typified the production of Welles's *Citizen Kane* (1941), the studio base of *Black Narcissus* therefore offered a challenge to artists and technicians. This gave opportunities to artists like Heckroth who were relatively unknown in the cinema, and also to composer Brian Easdale whose score for the film represented, according to Powell, their first experiments with 'the composed film'. Easdale had trained at the Royal College of Music and had little film experience before working on *Black Narcissus*, his first collaboration with Powell and Pressburger. Carol Reed recommended Easdale to Powell because he had worked with him on a documentary in India during the war. Another version of how Easdale became involved in the project contends that he knew Rumer Godden in India and arranged an appointment with Powell and Pressburger on his return to England after reading about their plans to adapt the novel for the screen.[55] Whatever its origins, their collaboration was successful, enabling Powell to experiment. Powell was keen to find a composer who 'thought operatically and whom I could entrust with all the sound effects for the film, as well as the music itself'.[56] The predominantly studio base of *Black Narcissus* thus presented Easdale with the opportunity to 'compose a sound-track which would be an organic whole of dialogue, sound effects, and music, very much in the way that opera is composed'.[57] In this way the 'musical sequence' which precedes Sister Ruth's fall to her death was composed as music before it was filmed. Powell recalls that they rehearsed and shot to a piano track:

> I insisted on rehearsing and shooting to a piano track and consulting Brian with a musical score in my hand over each set-up ... It was astonishing to everyone, but particularly, of course, to the camera crew that we were able to compress or speed up the movement of the action

just by saying: 'No that wasn't fast enough. We're only got seven seconds for that bit of action.'[58]

Jack Cardiff, however, does not remember there being any playback on the set.[59] Kathleen Byron greatly admired the music but told Brian McFarlane in 1990 that 'I didn't realise when I was stalking Deborah that there would be all that music to it'.[60] Presumably she is referring to the extent of the musical accompaniment, and there would have been precise timing on the sets anyway, but it is interesting that both Cardiff and Byron do not remember this aspect of the production being emphasised during shooting, at least not as explicitly as Powell later liked to recount. Easdale went on to work as musical director on many of The Archers' subsequent films, including *The Red Shoes*, for which he won an Academy Award. The shots, editing, creation of tone and mood are therefore holistic, a technique Powell experimented with further in *The Red Shoes* and *The Tales of Hoffmann* (1951).

CASTING

Mary Morris has already been mentioned as the actress who introduced Powell to the novel of *Black Narcissus* but who was never cast in her desired role of Sister Ruth. It was Powell's decision to give the part to Kathleen Byron, who had appeared as an officer angel in *A Matter of Life and Death*, even though Pressburger thought her not quite right for Sister Ruth.[61] He objected to Byron's insistence that Ruth was not insane but 'just a bit intense'. [62] In a record of Pressburger's corrections to the script he wrote, 'It must be emphasised she is ill all the time.'[63] In retrospect Byron's approach was judicious, since it would have been tempting to play Ruth in an exaggerated, over-melodramatic manner. Powell described Byron as having 'a dreamy voice and great eyes like a lynx' with 'the look of a zealot, a martyr', qualities that nevertheless produced a riveting portrayal of the disturbed Sister Ruth, emotionally unstable, but at the same time intelligent and calculating.[64]

The main female role of Sister Clodagh, the nun charged with leading the 'Convent of St Faith' at Mopu, was given to Deborah Kerr, the actress preferred by Pressburger but whom Powell considered to be too young (at one point Powell considered Greta Garbo for the role).[65] She had worked previously for Powell in a small part in *Contraband* and then played three different characters in *The Life and Death of Colonel Blimp*, an English governess in Berlin, a nurse in the First World War

who married 'Colonel Blimp' (Roger Livesey) and the driver of his
Home Guard unit car in the Second World War. To star in *Black
Narcissus* Kerr was loaned to The Archers from MGM at the start of
her Hollywood career. While working in Britain for producer Gabriel
Pascal she had been contracted to the American studio in 1943, and
Powell had to bargain hard for an affordable fee. The film's budget
breakdown shows, however, that Kerr's salary was by far the most
expensive: she was paid £16,000 for fifty-five days' work; David Farrar
was paid £4,500 for forty-five days; Flora Robson £3,100 for thirty-one
days and Kathleen Byron £900 for forty-four days.[66]

The major male lead role of the General's agent Mr Dean went to
David Farrar, a reporter-turned-stage actor who had been in several
British films, including *Went the Day Well?* (1942), *Meet Sexton Blake*
(1944) and *The Lisbon Story* (1946). The part of Dean was originally
intended to be played by Roger Livesey, and in January 1946 Robert
Donat was reading the script, but no firm decisions had been made.[67]
Powell noticed Farrar when visiting Elstree Studios and was struck by
his 'dark and saturnine good looks' and by the way he spoke 'a rather
artificial kind of BBC English'. He was asked to read the script and
screentest for the part and heard later that he had been successful. *Black
Narcissus* was a turning-point in his career: he considered the part of
Dean to be so good that he took it instead of signing a Hollywood
contract with Universal-International to play Grieg in *Song of Norway*.[68]
Flora Robson, an actress with a long-standing, distinguished reputation
on stage and screen, played Sister Philippa, the nun in charge of the
convent's garden, although at one time Pressburger thought of her as
suitable for Angu Ayah.[69] Several other important character actors were
present in the cast, including Judith Furse as Sister Briony and Nancy
Roberts as Mother Superior.

Sabu, an Indian actor, starred as the young General Dilip Rai, the
character who wears a perfume called 'Black Narcissus', purchased at
the Army and Navy Stores and which earns him the eponymous nick-
name, coined by the bitter and resentful Sister Ruth. While working as
an elephant driver in Mysore, south India, Sabu had been discovered at
the age of nine by Robert Flaherty when London Films were looking for
a lead actor for *Elephant Boy*. He went on to star in several other films
with imperial themes including *The Drum*, *The Thief of Bagdad* and *The
Jungle Book* (1942). Prem Chowdhry notes how the use of Technicolor
in films such as *The Drum* 'highlighted brilliantly the natural contrast of
the British and Indian skin colour, a contrast heightened by the image of

Sabu's bare torso'.[70] While this emphasised racial difference for Western audiences, Indian audiences reacted strongly against the film since 'the stark reality of their own humiliation, segregation and exploitation were never brought more forcefully to the fore than in the case of Sabu'.[71] When *The Drum* was exhibited in India it was greeted by severe criticism in the press and by protests in Bombay that eventually led to the film being withdrawn and later banned.[72] As for Sabu, he immediately became trapped into stereotypical roles, living out his 'rags to riches' destiny. Sabu went to live in America in the early 1940s, becoming a US citizen in 1944. By then a popular star, he took part in the US Treasury Department's 'defense-bond' sales campaign and served in the American Army Air Force. In the immediate post-war years his screen career had reached a low ebb, since none of the studios was planning a major imperial epic. Powell considered the part of the young General to be 'tailor-made' for Sabu and claims to have extended the role on hearing the news that Sabu had accepted the part.[73] As in his previous roles, however, Sabu played an amusing, somewhat childlike, supporting character.[74] Rumer Godden did not approve because although Sabu had charm she considered it to be 'deliberately blind' to cast 'a thick-set, snub-nosed South Indian coolie boy as a young Rajput prince'.[75] Sabu was in fact twenty-four years old when he played the young General, this remark confirming the prevalence of the 'trope of infantalisation' that was common within colonialist discourse as a means of projecting 'the colonised as embodying an earlier stage of individual human or broad cultural development'.[76]

Jean Simmons, a young actress who had been successful in *Caesar and Cleopatra* and *Great Expectations* (1946) and had aspirations towards Hollywood stardom, appeared as the Indian woman Kanchi who does not speak a word of dialogue yet, as the pressbook insisted, 'dominates every sequence in which she appears'.[77] This, and other casting, provides an interesting example of non-Indians performing such roles (May Hallatt as Angu Ayah is also a 'pretend native', as is Esmond Knight as the old General), while the young General and Joseph Anthony (Eddie Whaley Jr), the Indian boy who helps out at the school, are played by non-white actors.[78] While depicted as mischievous and in league with Mr Dean, Angu Ayah is cast in the much the same mould as Sabu and Joseph Anthony – as a comic, rather childlike character who at times is embarrassing to watch. Yet arguably her appearance and portrayal, as with Esmond Knight's old General, is an obvious and 'amusing' masquerade. May Hallatt was an established character actress associated with playing 'eccentric' roles such as this. As the old General is first seen closely when he is admiring himself in a mirror, dressed in elaborate clothes and speaking loftily of his invitation to the nuns to come to the palace, Kanchi is later seen dancing in front of the same mirror, evoking similar associations with vanity and a regard for opulent costume. At the time this employment of British actors was common practice in films set in imperial contexts and even subsequently, for example Alec Guinness appears 'blacked-up', in *A Passage to India* as late as 1984. Extras for crowd scenes were, however, procured from the local London Asian population who, according to Powell, were encouraged to bring their own costumes.[79]

The pressbook's discussion of Jean Simmons's passing as Kanchi concentrated on her ability as a versatile actress to carry off this unusual feat, especially since her last role had been as Estella in *Great Expectations*, in which she had been required to be 'haughty and aloof', whereas as Kanchi she had to 'personify feminine allure'.[80] Powell described Kanchi as 'the young Indian girl who brings the world, the flesh, and the devil into the nuns' retreat'.[81] In this conception her sexually charged dances and sensual, desiring glances confirm a stereotype of voracious 'native' sexual appetites and associations with primitivism, a view confirmed when the young General runs off with Kanchi, abandons his ambitions to go to Cambridge and settles instead for life as a prince with a harem. Rumer Godden approved of the casting of Jean Simmons, recording in her autobiography that she 'perfectly fulfilled my description'.[82] While many of these stereotypes might seem offensive to present-day audiences, it is important to note that they were in keeping with contemporary representations. Godden's satisfaction with Kanchi, based on her original conception of the character, testifies to the extent to which such representations were taken for granted as being 'authentic', ironically all the more so because they were played by white actors who had no qualms about exaggerating their roles. As argued in Chapter Two, the stereotypes in *Black Narcissus* are none the less complex in their degrees of agency, in some cases demonstrating a shift of emphasis in the dominant codes evident in earlier empire films.

PRODUCTION

The main period of shooting was from 16 May to 22 August 1946.[83] Junge's sets were elaborate and extensive, employing many ingenious ways in which to create the Himalayas at Pinewood. The old palace was built high above other buildings and trees, surrounded by a wall of planks and inclining at an angle of thirty-five degrees. This created a slope that would banish shadows, meaning that shooting could take place throughout the day.[84] The 'mountain', complete with terraces and winding pathways, was built on scaffolding, 120 feet high and strengthened by sleepers which formed 'stilts' or a framework for the set. These were then covered with prefabricated plaster or cement sheets to create the effect of natural rock. The 'mountain' was then filled in with gravel and soil and the terraces planted with quick-growing seeds.[85] This structure was so strong that it could withstand the weight of horses. Percy Day and his team painted the mountains and other scenic shots that were used for the atmospheric backgrounds. As Lightman explains:

> The elaborate backdrops used were skillfully painted in glowing colors and set up against the sky to hide the well-tended shrubbery of the English countryside. The enormous sheets of painted canvas were set at an angle of 30 degrees from the vertical in order to catch the sunlight for a longer period of time and thus prolong the hours when shooting was possible each day.[86]

Alfred Junge prepared for his set designs by creating clay models of the entire palace, carefully considering that each room had to be seen to undergo some kind of change, from its original use to occupation by the nuns. In so doing he had to create an overall impression of conflict, a sense of 'atmospheric struggle between the "old" and the "new"', with the *old* gradually winning out as the jungle creeps in on the cultivated patch'.[87] When he was designing Sister Clodagh's office he decided – on the basis of examining old Indian prints and paintings – it was likely that the room would have originally been used as an aviary. So, at the beginning of the film we see the room filled with birdcages and birds flying around before it is transformed into an office with only an overhead structure and the odd remaining bird to remind us of its former function. Junge's designs were striking in their imaginative conception, but departed from Godden's image of India. Godden's palace was simpler and plainer than Junge's – one storey high, 'its roof came down close to the ground and it had no open verandahs; every space had a thick glass pane'.[88] By contrast, Junge designed windows that were partially covered with a latticed criss-cross pattern, a device that Powell used to great effect when showing characters watching people and events outside. In several such shots the creation

7. *Kanchi and the young General in the 'Blue Room' with erotic wall paintings.*

of a diamond-shaped frame within a frame privileged voyeuristic looks that undoubtedly add to the film's overall structures of suspense. But when Godden saw the finished film she disapproved of Junge's elaborations of her descriptions, criticising his vision of the palace at Mopu as 'a ramshackle imitation of the pavilion in Brighton'.[89] Junge did, however, use Godden's description of blue walls for the central room with a sofa in the middle. It is this room where both the old General and later Kanchi admire themselves in the mirror and where Kanchi performs a sensual dance; its opulence suggests a defiant reminder of the palace's past. (See illustration 7 of Kanchi and the young General in the blue room.) In this way, despite Godden's objections, the film stayed true to a consistent sense of visual style that was appropriate in a cinematic context.

Jack Cardiff had to take care to create a balance between his own desire to experiment with Technicolor and the need to placate the overseeing supervision of Natalie Kalmus. Her ex-husband, Herbert Kalmus, had established Technicolor in the USA in 1915, and Natalie Kalmus's job was to make sure that once developed, the process was used 'properly', demanding 'a luridly chromatic palette, with flat, even lighting. Anything approaching chiaroscuro, or deliberate variation of exposure, was forbidden.'[90] Her presence caused Cardiff some anxiety, since he wanted in some scenes to use muted colour and fog filters, a diffusing technique not readily approved of by Technicolor but which he had already utilised on *A Matter of Life and Death*. A striking example of this is the scene when a tired and distraught Sister Clodagh goes to ring the bell towards the end of the film, just before she is attacked by Sister Ruth. In this scene and others Cardiff recalls that he went ahead with his tonal experiments, and was guided by a 'painterly' imperative, drawing on the expressive tones of Van Gogh and the greens and reds of Rembrandt's paintings. Other painters who were influential were Vermeer and Caravaggio. Cardiff's use of low-key lighting was remarkable, using few or no fill lights to produce expressionist effects not normally used for Technicolor. As Cardiff explained: 'They both lit with very simple light. Many painters did, but with Vermeer and Caravaggio you were very conscious of it; they really used the shadows. Caravaggio would just have one sweeping light over everything so that you were aware of the single light.'[91]

When the rushes were screened, Natalie Kalmus appreciated what Cardiff was trying to achieve and withdrew her objections.[92] The entire production was a technical challenge, not least because of having to manoeuvre the Technicolor cameras, which were extremely cumbersome because of their unwieldy soundproofing casings ('blimps'). A wind machine was used to create the breeze that is so important as a persistent, invasive element in the film. Some shots/scenes were not included in the final release print, particularly a scene at the end of the film when Sister Clodagh returns to Calcutta, which Cardiff considered his best work for the film. This will be discussed in the next chapter's detailed analysis of *Black Narcissus*, but it is sufficient to note here that Pressburger, who usually supervised the editing, appears to have exercised a high degree of creative control at this stage.[93]

The transition from novel to film had therefore taken place in a relatively short period of time, between 1945 and 1947. The production benefited from a source novel that lent itself well for screen adaptation by Powell and Pressburger (both worked on the screenplay) and Jack Cardiff's skills with Technicolor cinematography. Powell's clear directorial vision, supported by the excellent technical team and cast, produced a film remarkable on many levels, not least for the timing of its release. While there is no evidence to suggest that the eve of Indian independence was a contributory factor in The Archers' decision to make the film, the coincidence is strikingly prescient.[94] This creative triumph of artifice can be seen as a fascinating cultural meditation on the end of empire. The final lines of the novel provide a poignant summary of the conflicts contained within its pages, conflicts that Powell and Junge exaggerated in the design of the film:

> They were all startled by a sudden clap of thunder that went roaring down the hill.
>
> 'Dear goodness we must hurry! That's the rain.'
>
> The grooms sprang up, stamping the fire out. The Sisters rose stiffly, brushing leaves and moss from their habits.
>
> Sister Clodagh put the cup back on the tray.[95]

The environment has defeated them; it appears to hasten their departure. The thunder roars, the fire must be stamped out and the leaves and moss that have dishevelled their habits swept away. The cup is put back on the tray; order and propriety have apparently been restored. But the problems the nuns experienced have been signalled as ones that cannot so easily be dismissed. As we shall see in the next chapter, the film highlights these troubling aspects in very particular ways that contribute to its ability to elaborate strands of Godden's novel with striking, visual imagery.

TWO
Analysis

Powell and Pressburger's script kept fairly close to the basic episodic
details of Godden's novel: in terms of structure, the two are similar
in that they broadly deal with the nuns' arrival in Mopu; their difficult
period of acclimatisation and increasing reliance on Mr Dean, the arrival
and establishment of two key figures, the young General and Kanchi;
the gradual unsettling of the nuns' priorities and the intervention of
memories from their pasts; Sister Ruth's increasing instability; a major
mistake in the dispensary involving cultural misunderstanding; a climactic scene when Sister Ruth goes missing, is rejected by Mr Dean and
then tries to kill Sister Clodagh at the bell tower, but falls to her death
in the struggle and, finally, the nuns leaving Mopu as the rains break.
The following analysis will concentrate on the film but references the
novel where appropriate. While the two texts are structurally similar,
on several occasions they differ. This presents an interesting comparison
in terms of how novel and film locate themselves as colonial/post-
colonial texts. It will be argued that from many perspectives the film
represents a far more unstable vision of empire, perhaps explained
by the eight years that separate the publication of the novel (1939)
and the release of the film (1947). Even more important, however,
is the film's intense visualisation of the East as an environment that
cannot be safely contained as a backdrop for adventure and conquest.[1]
Rather, it is represented as a remarkable, topographic structure that is
alien to the nuns' experience but at the same time strangely familiar
in terms of its capacity to re-engage them with memories of the past
and sexuality. On a broader level, this troubling of binary divisions
between East and West locates *Black Narcissus* as a meditation on the
complex dynamics of de-colonisation that equates with Homi Bhabha's
ideas about cultural hybridity and the contested legacy of imperialism.
In particular it reveals the extent to which a post-colonial perspective
is evident in a film that deals with the waning of empire: out of the

persistence of the colonial past the present is inflected with a haunting resonance, creating gaps and fissures, instances of what Bhabha would term 'disjunctive enunciation'.[2]

THE ESTABLISHMENT OF ST FAITH

From the very start of the film it is notable that place and atmosphere are privileged above anything else. The opening shot – a close-up of two Tibetan ceremonial horns – shows dominant circular shapes in the centre of the screen with a vivid blue-sky background. The next shot reveals that they are erected on a hoist, blown by men in Eastern costume, followed by a series of (painted) shots showing the mountains, while the film's titles are presented. This close-up of the horns appears again fairly soon, when we first see Sister Ruth ringing the bell that has been appropriated by the newly established convent as a time-keeper. In this second appearance of the horns we hear them at the same time as the sound of the ringing bell – two sounds, and ways of living – momentarily co-existing in and around Mopu. Perhaps they are in competition: the strident horns indicating Eastern tradition and permanence and the bell that regulates the Sisters' activities in the same way as it would had they been in their 'home' convent in England. This opening is therefore important in creating a sense of permanence, presented in an assertive and dominating manner: the place, its sounds and traditions are signalled as being inviolable. The basic juxtaposition of sights and sound announces not only the film's major thematic contrast but also a stylistic technique that is used on several subsequent occasions. It illustrates how a few sentences from the novel were transposed to the screen with great effect. Godden wrote of the incongruity of a time-keeping bell in Mopu: 'Here the bell did not command, it sounded doubtful against the gulf; the wind took the notes away and yet it brought the sound of the bells at Goontu very strongly; pagan temple bells.'[3] While Godden's contrast with the convent's bell is 'pagan' bells, Powell chose to use the Tibetan horn for this purpose, a more visually striking symbol of the East.

The novel begins with the nuns arriving at Mopu, before explaining how the convent came to be established there, similarly emphasising from the outset the place and a sense of intrusion by people from a different culture. The following 'back-story' of Sister Clodagh's appointment as the nun placed in charge of St Faith and the reasons for the choice of Sisters who accompany her, provided Powell and Press-

8. *Jack Cardiff's Vermeer-inspired lighting structure in the classroom scene in Calcutta.*

burger with the opportunity to create a stark sense of visual contrast with the opening shots of the horns being played and the mountains. Jack Cardiff's use of expressionist low-key lighting and muted colour (blue/mauve whites and dark greys predominate) is noticeable in the scene announced as 'Convent of the Order of the Servants of Mary, Calcutta'. A scenario of order and regimentation is presented as Reverend Mother/Mother Dorothea (Nancy Roberts) looks out of the window of a room that has an institutional air with its dominating horizontal and vertical lines, with a fan spinning on the ceiling to regulate the heat. Jack Cardiff's *hommage* to Vermeer's paintings is clearly visible: the most dominant light source is strong beams streaming in through a window to illuminate an interior, a technique also used in the next scene when Sister Clodagh is called from her classroom to see Reverend Mother (see illustration 8 – classroom).[4] There follows between them a close, tense scene that is ostensibly informational, yet provides the occasion for our first sustained scenes of Mopu. The theme of contrasting locales is again emphasised as Mopu and its environs come to life when Reverend Mother shows Clodagh a letter from Mr Dean

(David Farrar), the Agent of General Toda Rai (Esmond Knight) who has invited them to establish the convent. As Dean's voiceover tells us about Mopu and the mountains we then dissolve to the place and learn from him about its ways and people.

We are aware that his version of Mopu as 'the back of beyond' is partial and biased. His descriptions of the people, for example, are somewhat patronising when he refers to them as 'like mountain peasants everywhere – simple, independent', illustrated by *National Geographic*-style close-up shots of men, women and children. Dean maintains this singular view of the local people throughout, even though he claims to have had extensive experience in dealing with them through his work. But gradually his voiceover fades, and we are allowed to see the place in a less overtly directed fashion. There are brief scenes with the Holy Man, a silent, spiritual figure who meditates on the hillside; Angu Ayah (May Hallat), the caretaker of the palace; Mr Dean and the General. Mr Dean and Angu Ayah treat the General's hopes for the success of the nuns' mission with scepticism when they predict that it will fail. As the camera follows Angu Ayah it surveys the palace where we see Junge's erotic wall painting designs, which communicate a sense of its past as the 'House of Women', a perspective that could not have been envisaged by Reverend Mother and Sister Clodagh since its function is, for the viewer, outside the containing structure of Mr Dean's voiceover. This is different from the novel, in which we learn that Clodagh visited Mopu a month before her interview with Mother Superior and that she was affected by it: 'She had not forgotten it since. It was extraordinary how she had remembered it; the feeling of the house and the strange thoughts she had when the General's agent, Mr Dean, showed them over it. It had reminded her of Ireland. Was it the unaccustomed greenness, or the stillness of the house after the wind outside?'[5] This early mention of how Mopu reminds Clodagh of her past is the first suggestion of a blurring of past and present, of East and West, that becomes so important for the film and the function of its subsequent flashbacks.

Priya Jaikumar has noted that this particular introduction to Mopu is typical of the film's more general unsettling presentation of place. She argues that this illustrates the extent to which *Black Narcissus* differs from previous British films with imperial settings, such as *Sanders of the River* (1935), *The Drum* and *The Four Feathers*, which construct 'place' very much as a mere backdrop for colonialist concerns:

The distance between the viewer and the place, created by our sense that the three characters [Mr Dean, Reverend Mother and Sister Clodagh] are imagining Mopu, combined with our knowledge of their relationships to the place and the mission, debilitates the containment of Mopu within any singular perspective. These narrative and cinematic techniques mark the film as presenting fragmented realities, separating it significantly from films in other modes of the imperial imagination in which the presentations of place are strenuously singular.[6]

Jaikumar describes *Black Narcissus* as a 'modernist' imperial text in which the colonial backdrop is constructed as problematic. In this case, she argues, 'a colonial place is made central enough to impede the assumptions projected onto it'.[7] It is ironic that this centrality of place was achievable because of Powell's decision not to shoot the film in India: the 'East' that was compelling, beguiling and seductive was in fact the creation of Western imagination. The principle of centrality is none the less a key element of the film's realisation of Godden's vision.

A sense of complexity surrounding Mopu is also communicated by the wind that blows through the palace because of its high position. As Godden described in the novel:

To step into the house was to step into stillness, into warmth even when it was damp and unlit; but after a moment a coldness crept about your shins. The wind could not be kept out of the house; it came up through the boards of the floor and found passages between the roof and the ceiling cloths; at Mopu Palace you lived with the sound of the wind and a coldness always about your ears and ankles.[8]

Brian Easdale's soundtrack uses choral strains as an appropriate accompaniment for the wind blowing through the 'House of Women' harbouring, as Mr Dean puts it, 'the ghosts of bygone days'. In addition, the sound of the wind is therefore invested with associations of the past function of the palace. Easdale's choral strains become important signifiers of female sexuality. The harem of the past is not depicted as an oppressive place for the women but instead, as indicated by the paintings which almost appear to become animated by the choral soundtrack, as a locus of pleasure and eroticism. Its contrasting usage by the nuns, as Mr Dean and Angu Ayah point out, could not be more different and their anticipated defeat is, by implication, acknowledgement that the 'place' is impervious to Western influence. During their occupation of the palace the nuns attempt to convert it into a religious house, but

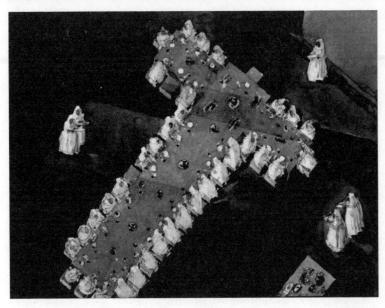

9. *Alfred Junge's drawing for the high overhead shot of the nuns' dining table in Calcutta. Sister Ruth's place is empty.*

10. *Still from the film of the same scene showing the exactitude of the drawings.*

the permanence of the wall paintings and the incessant wind serve as constant reminders of the place and its past.

The film then reverts to Calcutta and follows fairly closely the novel's descriptions of the nuns who are to accompany Clodagh in the establishment of St Faith. We learn that theirs is a voluntary Order – the nuns take their vows annually – a fact that becomes important later when Sister Ruth declares that she wants to leave. The voluntary nature of the Order also introduces a key element of choice that becomes crucial in heightening the sense of emotional disturbance they feel when challenged by a seductive, yet alien environment: as such there are no sanctions – except moral – against them choosing to leave St Faith. In a scene shot from above as Clodagh and Mother Superior look down on the nuns at dinner sitting at a cross-shaped table, we are given a quick guide to their strengths and in so doing are introduced to the actresses with a series of brief character sketches (see figures 9 and 10 – Junge's drawing of the table and still from the film. Both show Ruth's empty place.) Sister Briony (Judith Furse) is chosen for her strength; Philippa (Flora Robson) for her gardening talents; Blanche (known as 'Sister Honey', played by Jenny Laird) for her popularity and Ruth (Kathleen Byron) is presented as a kind of challenge. We do not see her – she is represented by her empty place at the table – an unusual, but appropriate introduction for such an important character. We hear that she is troubled but, according to Mother Superior, could improve if given responsibility, an opinion not entirely shared by Clodagh. Mother Superior reprimands her for this, warning her against feeling too important and repeating the novel's line, 'Remember the Superior of all is the servant of all.'[9] The severity of her opinion that Clodagh is not ready for the task, warning her that she will be lonely, comes across more harshly in the film than in the novel, in which Mother Superior is given an important line that softens her character when she tells Clodagh not to forget to enjoy herself. In their adaptation Powell and Pressburger must have felt that this softer approach was not appropriate for the film, in which Clodagh is established as proud and rather stubborn.

The following scenes return us to Mopu with a close-up shot of huge double doors that fill the frame. A nun walks into this striking image; we see her from behind, opening the great doors with her habit blown by the wind as she walks out towards the bell. This establishes a recurring visual strategy used by Powell when we are shown many instances of doors and windows, frequently creating frames within a

11. *Ruth ringing the bell.*

frame. On a metaphorical level these motifs can be interpreted as attempts to control the environment, to contain its disturbing elements within habitable structures. Yet we also are constantly reminded of how the wind nevertheless blows incessantly through the palace, of its failure to protect the nuns from outside forces. The contrast with Reverend Mother's office, with its pulsating fan and *mise-en-scène* of order, could not be greater. The camera remains behind the nun who has opened the doors until we infer that it is Ruth, whom so far we have not seen but who now has her own distinctive visual introduction, ringing the bell. This association between Ruth and the bell is important in establishing imagery that will recur throughout the film, linking this action with Ruth's desire to leave the Order (see illustration 11). The foregrounding of this imagery early on in the film is all the more important since Ruth is the character who is most affected by Mopu and who dies for her non-conformity. As the bell rings we also hear the horns sounding – the same horns that opened the film – creating the impression of two co-existing worlds.[10]

This scene is followed by introductions to the other nuns in their new Himalayan habitat: Philippa discussing the garden and referring to a book, looking at a page of vegetables and then turning it to look at flowers; Briony demonstrating a 'trick' by mixing potassium with water; Blanche starting up her lace school and the appointment of the young local boy 'Joseph Anthony' as their interpreter. His appearance is significant since it is the first inclusion of an 'outsider' into the convent. Like Mr Dean, Joseph Anthony is required for practical reasons and his acceptance signals the Sisters' need to adapt their convent to its locale. The precedent of taking in this young boy also makes it easier for Sister Clodagh to agree to allow the young General and Kanchi, a young woman brought to the convent by Mr Dean, to attend classes at St Faith, even though this is against her better judgement and is referred to later as contributing to their problems. It is the young General who reminds Clodagh of her past love, Con, and who triggers flashbacks to her life in Ireland before she became a nun. It is Kanchi who tempts the young General away from his studies and, in her physical similarity to the women in the erotic paintings, she is a constant reminder of the 'House of Women', even though the nuns try to transform the palace into the Convent of St Faith.

The 'settling in' period is also punctuated with some tetchy exchanges between Mr Dean and Sister Clodagh, as his knowledge of the place and its peoples is presented as a superior discourse which she is forced to acknowledge. His negative view of their chances of making a success of their mission immediately places him in the role of the observant sceptic when he pronounces: 'I'll give you until the rains break'. Defiantly, Clodagh tries to reduce the number of reminders of the palace's former function by insisting that one of the framed erotic pictures be taken down. What has initially been presented as an inappropriate place for a convent is then seen to be transformed, as indicators of

Christianity are placed in rooms while the school and dispensary take shape. Junge's sets are 'adapted' for habitation by the nuns as bearers of Western influence. Cardiff's cinematography explores these contrasts: in one such shot of Clodagh's room the camera pans across one of the erotic wall paintings to reveal its placement above a window and then we see how she has added an altar-like table, complete with candles and a cross hanging on the wall. These contrasting visual signifiers are key elements in establishing the film's central theme of missionary zeal exemplified by religious bodies which proselytised in the colonies and were complicit with imperialism. The very attempt to 'educate' local peoples underscores the strategy – as Homi Bhabha has observed – of creating 'a culturally and linguistically homogenous English India' that could be ruled with the assistance of educated Indians who acted as intermediaries between the colonialists and the colonised.[11] In the school no attempt is made to deliver anything but an 'English' education: in one scene Joseph Anthony teaches the students to identify in English the guns and weaponry associated with British imperialism by pointing to drawings of them on the blackboard: 'canon, warship, bayonet, dagger, gun'. The role of Joseph Anthony is littered with such uncomfortable moments as he performs the role of intermediary. The nuns need him as an interpreter, but he is verbally abused by Sister Ruth and forced to explain why the people have ostracised the dispensary after the incident of the sick baby. At the same time he is also accorded with insight and privileged information: he observes Kanchi's increasing attraction to the young General as he watches them secretly admire one another through the rudimentary partition dividing the lace and educational areas of the schoolroom. But his role is clearly a difficult one, appearing all the more poignant and awkward because he is a child.

In this way – and as Bagchi has noted about the novel – *Black Narcissus* is a fascinating text because at the same time as showing elements of the missionary zeal and its association with imperialism, it highlights the 'gaps, fissures, and slippages between colonial policy and its pursuit'.[12] The contradictions of the imperial position are made visible by the compromises Sister Clodagh has to make and by the awkwardness of many of the nuns' encounters with the young General, Kanchi, Joseph Anthony and the local people who attend the school and dispensary. While there is every attempt to treat the young General and Kanchi as if they were like the other students, they are marked by their costumes as different, more exotic, more distracting for the nuns and thus able to usurp them as a focus of fascination at Mopu. This illustrates the extent to which the nuns are unable to make their mark, of how their ambitions for St Faith are bound to be frustrated and how they cannot seal themselves off from their new, seductive and troubling environment. In this sense the confident dichotomies presented in earlier 'empire' films are challenged and troubled. As noted earlier, Rumer Godden objected to the overtly stylised costumes worn by the young General. Yet their function in the film is crucial in establishing him as an uncontrollable, distracting male/Eastern presence.

These questions of cultural ambivalence and of the 'unnatural' elements of imperialism are additionally drawn out by an incident the primary narrative function of which is to indicate Sister Ruth's instability and growing infatuation for Mr Dean. Mr Dean tells Sisters Clodagh and Briony that they should avoid dealing with serious cases in the dispensary since if a death occurred (as it does later on with disastrous consequences) they would be blamed. His reasons for this are that the people are 'primitive … like children … unreasonable', explaining their behaviour only in terms of Western cultural expectations. Yet he is warning them – perhaps in a way he thinks they will understand – against using the dispensary as an experiment in professionalism, telling them that they need to acknowledge local differences. At that moment Sister Ruth runs in, covered in blood, and tells them that she succeeded in stopping a wounded woman bleeding after some time of struggle. The association between Ruth and the colour red is established in a striking way since her habit is badly marked as visible evidence of the crisis. Red is later linked to her non-conformity when she wears a red dress and lipstick in place of her habit after having decided to leave the Order. In this scene she is proud that she stopped the bleeding, but is reprimanded by Clodagh for failing to fetch Sister Briony, who would have abated it much faster. This represents a conflict of interest between Ruth's desire to appear 'important' and the needs of the patient. In both Mr Dean's advice and Sister Ruth's behaviour there is a warning that compromises need to be made in terms of adapting to local understanding and of not using the dispensary for motives of personal aggrandisement or a demonstration of imperialist power. Sister Ruth is the nun who is consistently represented as being dismissive of local customs, although on this occasion it is significant that at the end of the scene Mr Dean thanks Ruth for her actions, an incident that contributes to her growing infatuation with him. In their different characterisations the nuns therefore represent a spectrum of the British in India: Ruth as the uncompromising imperialist; Briony as the professional who realises the limitations of their work; Blanche who wants the 'natives' to love her; Philippa who decides that being in Mopu is too powerful a distraction from her vocation; and Clodagh who realises only gradually that their work cannot be sustained. In this way both novel and film highlight the contradictions of the imperialist position as Mopu and its people displace notions of Western civilization and superiority.

The various 'native' characters in *Black Narcissus* are similarly representative of ambivalent attitudes towards colonialism. Joseph Anthony's awkward intermediate status between the nuns and the local people has already been referenced. Although Mr Dean describes them as being 'like children' they often possess key narrative functions. Angu Ayah, for example, is aligned with Mr Dean in that she shares his scepticism about the nuns making a success of their mission. It is implied that she is an eccentric, permanent fixture of the palace; she was there when it was 'The House of Women' and she will be there when the nuns leave (Mr Dean calls her 'a faithful, dirty old bird and goes with the place'). Our first sight of her is when we follow her through the rooms and corridors, her swaying movements almost replicating the wind that blows through the palace. She stands for the rejection of Western intervention, convinced that the people do not need a school or hospital. Wily and knowing, she encourages the young General to become involved with Kanchi when she invites him to beat her when she is accused of stealing. This has the opposite effect: it is the key event (he does not beat her; they end up in an embrace) when he decides to run off with her and abandon his aspirations for a Western education. We suspect that all along Angu Ayah wanted this to happen. In turn Kanchi is associated with sensuality and a natural form of sexuality. While this conforms to a Western stereotype of unsatiable sexual appetites and primitivism,[13] it is also contrasted with the nuns' repressed desires that in the case of Sister Ruth are presented as a hysterical illness, dangerous and ultimately tragic. Kanchi's role is therefore important in suggesting that sexuality can be liberated, uncomplicated and celebratory. On the other hand, the old General colludes with the colonial tradition of improvement: he wants the people to be educated by Westerners, an attitude shared by the young General who, until he runs off with Kanchi, has ambitions to go to Cambridge, appreciates Western fashions and declares that he is 'very much interested in Jesus Christ'. By contrast, the Holy Man is the General's uncle, who can speak several European languages and was decorated for his military achievements. He has, however, rejected

European influence as he sits on the hillside in constant meditation, a symbol of spirituality that disturbs Sister Clodagh. In his defence of the Holy Man Mr Dean suggests to Sister Clodagh that this form of worship is more in keeping with the 'true' teachings of Christ than is evident in organised religion. In this way a range of different perspectives on Western influence in India are present that complicate a straightforward interpretation of *Black Narcissus* as a classic colonial text. These examples of stereotypes being rendered unstable by the cultural 'Other' being negotiated link with Homi Bhabha's ideas about the inherent ambivalence of colonial authority because, as Kraniauskas explains, 'the very practice of enunciation, the discourse of culture itself, undermines any attempt at narrative closure or cultural self-constitution on the part of the subject of power'.[14]

MEMORY, DISPLACEMENT AND DISTURBANCE

Once the nuns have established St Faith the film develops the novel's idea that Mopu conjures up memories from the past. There is a definite association between the present and the past, as demonstrated by an indicative passage from the novel:

> [Clodagh] did not try to bother in these happy relaxed days, she simply let herself drift with the present or sink into the past. It was like practising the piano; at first your fingers feel cold and stiff, and the notes seem a little sharp on the air and the phrases stupid and meaningless. Then you are warm, it flows, it becomes music and it seems to take you where it flows. It was getting to be a habit with her, to let her mind flow away, to spend minutes and hours back in the past with Con.[15]

Powell and Pressburger take the cue from Godden to show characters in the present as instigators of flashbacks. As will be detailed later, it was Sister Clodagh's flashbacks that were the target of the US Catholic Legion of Decency's censorship campaign, a fact that draws attention to their function in the film. A link is established between Mopu and, in particular, the young General, and a love affair she had in Ireland before she joined the Order. As I have argued elsewhere, the first flashback evokes a particular association between the past and present that can be read as an attempt to collapse, or at least complicate, strict divisions between East and West.[16] Indeed, other aspects of the film work to complicate strictly binarist notions, as observed by Raymond Durgnat, who argued that 'The conflict[s] involve very complex patterns of opposites-and-equivalence. For East/West opposition is *dialecticised* through mediating figures … and by the recognition lurking under the exotic.'[17] The flashbacks in particular evoke an associative relationship between the past and the present (especially when introduced by dissolves and overlapping sounds), between Clodagh's memories of desire and her present exposure to such sensibilities: recognition induced by 'the exotic'. I stress the importance of the flashbacks because their troubling relationship between the past and present contributes to the film's overall unstable positioning in the canon of imperial fictions. Along with the general unsettling notion of place presented in the film, the flashbacks add a stark reminder of the futility of separating out time and space. While films that deploy flashbacks usually code them for the viewer as denoting the past by means of devices such as dissolves, it is also the case, as Maureen Turim has noted, that to some extent 'within a given flashback segment, the spectator experiences the film in exactly the same way that one experiences any other segment of a fiction film, as an ongoing series of events happening to the characters in their immediate temporal experience, that is in their "present"'.[18]

The introduction to the first flashback begins with an exterior shot of the palace, as Sister Philippa gives instructions about the garden and Ruth rings the bell lustily, in a manner similar to the way in which we have seen her perform this duty previously, as a high camera angle reveals the terrifying depth of the precipice. We then see Clodagh looking out of a window (the camera on the outside looking in), her eyes obscured by a shadow for a second as she says 'Hail Mary', this shot perhaps signalling the escalation of her temptation from duty as she notices that instead of doing her work in the garden, Sister Philippa is gazing towards the horizon.[19] Clodagh goes out and talks to Philippa in a scene in which we learn that she too is being distracted by the place, when Philippa admits that it conjures up thoughts from her past, commenting that you can 'see too far'. Clodagh agrees, blaming 'this place, with its strange atmosphere and new people'. We then move into the chapel, where Clodagh is praying, with the shadow of the cross over her face in a striking shot that communicates her dilemma. Choral sounds resonate on the soundtrack as she is clearly distracted from her prayer by the bright sky and foliage outside. Powell uses a dissolve to begin the flashback as we hear the words from the past, 'Isn't it a grand day, Con?' Thus begins an associative memory, triggered by the present. The beautiful scenery of a lake in Ireland where Con and Clodagh are fishing then becomes the main focus, a shimmering, glittering, landscape. It is surprising to see Clodagh, with her vivid red hair, looking relaxed as she stands up in the water fishing. She is no longer the proud nun with her hair covered up by a wimple. Her appearance in the flashback renders her exotic in comparison; in this regard East and West are similar. In this scene we learn that Clodagh wants to stay in Ireland, whereas Con cannot wait to leave. This divergence of opinion is communicated visually as well as aurally: when Con is speaking the static hillside in the background behind him is not as stunning as when Clodagh is speaking of her desire to remain there, with the shimmering, playful light on the water dancing behind her. We revert briefly to the present by means of a close-up dissolve of Clodagh's face in Ireland that appears to collapse into the present, her features matching exactly as the past merges into the present, in a shot that conveys her complete absorption in her memory before reverting again to the past, this time occasioned by the sound of a barking dog. We are then at a hunt scene – galloping horses with two riders singled out who, we assume, are Clodagh and Con. The camera follows the chase for some time in a location typical of Powell's affinity for pastoral scenes in a spectacular landscape. The present intrudes as we cut to the chapel, showing Clodagh totally enveloped by her memory, looking thrilled and happy but with the cross still in shadow over her face, as an aural connection is made between the sounds of the hunt and the arrival of the young General outside the palace on his horse. This sequence has a pleasing rhythmic quality to it, as do many of the scenes in *Black Narcissus*, very much engaging with Godden's sense of the past drifting into the present, her analogy to music and piano playing being singularly appropriate.[20]

The young General occasions Clodagh's third flashback, but this time when the nuns are discussing his elaborate and fascinating appearance. This association is taken from the novel, in which we learn that Clodagh perceives an incongruous yet compelling similarity between the young General and Con:

> She looked at him without speaking and tried to think just why it was he made her think of Con. She could hardly bear to look at him. Con had fair hair and a skin almost too white for a man but the quality of him was there in the young General waiting to speak to her. Con was in America; he was over forty, but she could not believe that. He was far more here, in this young Rajput, fumbling with his hat and gloves.[21]

When he attends the school he wears brightly coloured silks, jewels and the 'Black Narcissus' perfume, purchased at the Army and Navy Stores.[22] In contrast to the rugged masculinity represented by Mr Dean, the young General reacquaints the nuns with an appreciation for sartorial elegance, visual splendour and physical beauty. Clodagh listens to Sister Blanche's detailed description of yet another sumptuous costume worn to school by the young General. At the mention of emeralds she is reminded of her grandmother's footstool, as we cut to a shot of a footstool and Clodagh being shown an emerald necklace that her grandmother intends to give to her when she marries. She tries it on and looks at herself in a mirror with pleasure before taking it off hastily when she hears Con whistle outside, waiting for her to go out with him. She opens the front door and runs out to meet him, but instead of us seeing him greet her she runs out into the night, the frame gradually enveloped by black. This perhaps prefigures his literal disappearance from her life, a sign of her dashed hopes for marriage. The fourth flashback follows quite soon afterwards and is occasioned by memories of Christmas. Clodagh is in the chapel, when the carol 'Lullay My Liking' reminds her of Con giving her a brooch at Christmas. These incidents, it can be argued, are examples of a Freudian 'return of the repressed', that Michael Walker cites as being a key element of *Black Narcissus*.[23] Clodagh's memories of romance, sexuality and longing are summoned forth by Mopu in a complex way that introduces tension, since we know that these private moments are inappropriate in her current situation as a nun. Our sharing of them with her gives the audience a privileged perspective on her character and current dilemma.

It is significant that all four flashbacks deal with pleasurable moments from the past, yet within these there are signs that Clodagh will not attain the future she desires. We later learn that she entered the Order when it became clear that Con was going to America without taking her with him. This conclusion to Clodagh's back-story is not communicated in a flashback, but when she confides in Mr Dean at a vulnerable moment when the nuns' problems at St Faith have escalated and shortly before Sister Ruth escapes. Unaware that Ruth is watching this intimate conversation, she confesses: 'I've been drifting and dreaming and now I seem to be living through the struggle and the bitterness again.' It might appear to be inconsistent that while the Legion of Decency's recommended cuts included all the flashbacks, they did not excise the scene between Clodagh and Mr Dean when she tells him that she has been haunted by her past and that a failed love affair led her to join the Order ('I loved a man … I had shown him I loved him').[24] Presumably the flashbacks' visual force was considered to be more dangerous than the mere knowledge that Clodagh had a romantic past. While the novel has both – passages on which the flashbacks in the film are based, and the scene in which Clodagh tells Mr Dean about her past – the film's censorship reveals the extent to which visual images were considered to be more affecting than information about the past communicated in dialogue. In the flashbacks Deborah Kerr's physical beauty is particularly striking: as we have seen she is presented as lively and attractive, in contrast with her dutiful, more serious demeanour as a nun, wearing a habit that hides her vibrant red hair. As well as the seductiveness of the visual pleasures contained in the flashbacks, their timing is also of key significance in trying to understand this apparent contradiction in the Legion's actions. They all come before the nuns begin to experience their most serious problems at Mopu, and are therefore placed in a context in which they indeed appear to be compelling, exciting and in some ways preferable to the present. The scene between Clodagh and Mr Dean occurs much later, after the baby has died, the people no longer come to the school and dispensary, and after Sister Philippa has declared that she must leave Mopu. Mr Dean advises them to leave since 'there's something in the air that makes everything seem exaggerated'. By this time any confession Clodagh makes to Mr Dean is overshadowed by her vulnerability and the knowledge that their work has been adversely affected by the seductions of 'place' and memory. She explicitly admits to being totally distracted by the environment: 'I had to take in the young General, I couldn't turn out the Holy Man. I couldn't stop the wind from blowing and the air from being as clear as crystal, and I couldn't hide the mountain.' Her profound sense of failure comes at a moment when she begins to accept that they must leave, a feeling that is confirmed when Sister Ruth disappears in pursuit of Mr Dean.

FEMININITY, SEXUALITY AND THE PROBLEM OF SISTER RUTH

The Legion of Decency's insistence that Sister Clodagh's flashbacks be cut for the American print draws attention to their compelling visual imagery of the nun without a habit, of the film star looking her best, of romance and sexuality. The treatment of Sister Ruth also highlights these themes of contrast, which are so important in escalating the film's sense of dramatic and emotional suspense. As well as the flashbacks, the

Legion objected to Sister Ruth's transformation from the brooding nun to the desirous vamp in the scene when she puts on lipstick in front of Sister Clodagh. This melodramatic aspect is not in the novel: Ruth does not obtain ordinary clothes; she does not 'dress up' in preparation for her pursuit of Mr Dean. Above all, the film's reputation for being risqué resides in the spectacle of the nun divested of her robes, behaving in a sexually rapacious manner and having no respect for her superiors. In this way the film highlights a fascination with femininity and sexuality and in particular emphasises that Ruth is what Clodagh fears she herself might become if she does not stifle her memories of the past and the unsettling feelings she has experienced at Mopu.

As a device, flashbacks introduce narrational complexity.[25] They also assist in reinforcing the audience's identification with a particular character (the one who has the flashback) since they provide access to another time-frame, another life. As the nun in charge of the Order, Sister Clodagh's role is important as a sensible woman who represents stability. Knowledge of her past threatens to shatter this position of authority and responsibility, indicating that in many respects she is as vulnerable as Sister Ruth, whose function in the film is to represent hysterical, rebellious femininity. From this perspective Ruth represents what Clodagh might easily become: disturbed and uncontrollable, a figure of threatening madness. Priya Jaikumar has also noticed how 'Sister Ruth is arguably a distended reflection of all the weaknesses and deviances that the nuns, and particularly Sister Clodagh, experience in their encounter with (and responses to) Mopu'.[26] Michael Walker even goes so far as to argue that Ruth represents in dramatic form Clodagh's repressed sexual desire for Mr Dean and that in seeking to reform her, Clodagh is struggling to control the dangerous, unconscious urges she herself has been experiencing.[27]

Clodagh is established as somewhat vulnerable from the start. As we have seen, she is considered to be too young, too proud, not ready for the responsibility of being in charge of St Faith. In our first introduction to her, Mother Superior casts her in this position, as her youth is contrasted with the older nun's severe manner and authoritative demeanour. The design of the wimples emphasises the age difference between the nuns, fully revealed by alternate close-ups of their faces, with the wimple acting as a framing device. While Mother Superior's face is lined and sagacious, Clodagh's skin is young, fresh and clear. The heightening effect of Technicolor tended to redden the actresses' lips, so much so that they had to wear pale lipstick to lessen this result.

But in these early shots of Clodagh the reddish tint is evident, which adds to her identity as the young ingénue whom the audience also recognises as a famous film star. The characterisation of Clodagh as inexperienced continues at Mopu when she is beholden to the local, practical knowledge that only Mr Dean possesses, and learns to rely on his judgement until by the end of the film his prediction that they will stay only 'until the rains break' is vindicated.

The inclusion of Sister Ruth in the mission is presented as a potential problem from the start. As noted earlier, Clodagh is visibly disturbed at the thought of her accompanying them to Mopu, and Mother Superior points to a similarity between them when she replies to Clodagh's objection that Ruth ought not to be given 'importance' by pointing out that Clodagh must spare her some of her own importance. It is as if Ruth is Clodagh's embarrassment, her disturbing *alter ego*, something that Mother Superior can see and which is part of Clodagh's test. Every encounter between them is premised on conflict. Ruth is presented as being rebellious, racist (she is the only nun who makes overt remarks criticising the local people; she objects to Joseph Anthony, the young General and Kanchi) and unstable. The scenes of her ringing the bell encapsulate her predicament. They are clearly coded as sexual by the lusty way in which she pulls the rope and by the excited expression on her face that prefigures her pursuit of Mr Dean. Kathleen Byron was keen to play Ruth as 'intense' but not mad, although Powell and Pressburger clearly enhanced this view of her in the scenes when she stalks Clodagh leading up to the climactic scene at the bell tower.[28] After her transformation, her struggle through the valley to Mr Dean's place, his rejection of her and her return to St Faith, we see her white, stark face that reminds us of a horror film, before she tries to push Clodagh over the precipice.[29]

A key confrontational scene illustrates the energy of the film's formal construction and its ability to replicate characters' emotions. When Clodagh tells Ruth of her concern about her and broaches the question of her infatuation with Mr Dean, the camera focuses on Ruth's hand, holding a pencil she breaks when Clodagh remarks that Ruth is 'thinking too much of Mr Dean'. Immediately before panning up from the hand to reveal Ruth's facial reaction, the camera momentarily focuses on a Bible in acknowledgement of their status as nuns – nuns who have succumbed to passionate feelings.[30] We then see Ruth's face, full of anger in recognition that Clodagh has hit on the truth, retorting with how pleased Clodagh also appears to be at the sight of Mr

Dean. Byron thought that the force of this was too extreme: 'Michael wanted me to say it right across the table, in a quite grotesque position, almost as if suddenly the devil had popped out. I didn't think it was necessary but that was how he wanted it done.'[31] Nevertheless, it is highly effective. The force of the impact of this devastating remark on Clodagh is visually punctuated by her abruptly standing up – appearing almost to jump into the frame on hearing this shocking statement.[32] This establishes intensity between the two women that returns in the 'transformation' scene described below and again towards the end of the film when Ruth stalks Clodagh.

The 'transformation' scene that illustrates the explosive tension between the two women is remarkable for its expressionist lighting, use of close-ups and colour. The sequence begins with men beating drums, sitting in a circle in the valley below the convent. Drums are a signifier in colonial films of 'otherness' and impending danger. In this context they establish an association between Sister Ruth's rebellious sexual awakening and primitivism that returns when she later escapes in pursuit of Mr Dean. We continue to hear the drums as we see Clodagh walking down the dark corridor at night, holding a candle. She knocks on Sister Ruth's door and when she gets no response we see that inside Ruth has barricaded herself in by propping a chair against the door. Clodagh knocks again and as she does so, the door opens and we see the startling vision of Ruth not wearing her habit, dressed in a dark reddish dress and wearing red lipstick. Her dramatic new appearance is aurally punctuated by Easdale's rising choral soundtrack and her strident proclamation that Clodagh cannot order her about any more, that she has nothing to do with her. Clodagh tries to placate her by saying that she wants to send her back to the Order with Sister Philippa, who has requested to be transferred, only to be met with protestations from Ruth that she won't be silenced. The low-key lighting emphasises the horror elements of the scene when Ruth's figure is shot against the criss-cross pattern of the window with the deep blue sky intruding from outside. Clodagh decides to stay with Ruth, whose stark white face is further contrasted with her red lips as she puts on more lipstick in front of Clodagh (see illustration 12). To emphasise the intensity of her rebellion Powell uses an extreme close-up shot of her lips and then pans up to her eyes as they fixate on Clodagh. At this moment Clodagh takes up her Bible, as if to ward off the evil aura Ruth has unleashed. The candle burning lower and lower is intercut with details from the erotic wall paintings, emphasising the link between the effect of the

12. *Ruth putting on lipstick in front of Clodagh, who retaliates by getting out her Bible.*

place and Ruth's physical and emotional transformation. As Clodagh drops off to sleep Ruth excitedly puts on her boots and picks up a pair of red shoes.[33] The candle goes out, Clodagh awakens and Ruth runs out, laughing maniacally as she shuts the door behind her, preventing Clodagh from following her immediately. As Ruth runs down the corridor she brushes past a statue of the Hindu god Shiva (associated with destruction), dislodging the lace cover that had been placed over it, as if she has now fully unleashed all the forces that will defeat the nuns. As Clodagh looks out of the window the pattern of the lattice is reflected on her habit and the search for Ruth begins. It is as if Clodagh is also tainted, the 'marked' habit a visual signifier of her loss of control and the connection of her fate with Ruth (in subsequent scenes we see that the cloak over her habit has literally become sullied in the desperate search for Ruth). The intensity of this scene has further established a link between the two women that brings out the full complexities of the film's meditation on female sexuality. It is so erotically charged that Andrea Weiss re-edited it and used another soundtrack in her gay and lesbian film *A Bit of Scarlet* (1994), discussed later in this book.

The film's presentation of femininity is clearly condemnatory of Ruth's out-and-out pursuit of Mr Dean. Sexuality is associated with being out of control: in this context representing an excessive 'primitive' Eastern physicality associated with the sensuous exchanges between the young General and Kanchi. A striking example of this is when Ruth has escaped and goes to see Mr Dean in his hut in the valley, down below the convent. We hear the incessant beating of drums, as in the earlier scene just before Ruth appears in her ordinary clothes for the first time, thus repeating the link between her rebellion and the influence of 'the East'. As a small, vulnerable figure surrounded by huge bamboo trees in the dark valley, Ruth appears to be in an alien environment, bewildered and out of her depth (see illustration 13). This is emphasised by the stark change in the musical soundtrack from the drums to a calmer, more lyrical string theme as she enters the hut, as if she has arrived at a safe and familiar haven as she surveys Mr Dean's living quarters, looking at his belongings lovingly and picking up his pipe (the latter could of course be interpreted as a gesture with sexual connotations).[34] Interestingly, in the novel Ruth's encounter with Mr Dean takes place in the factory, so it does not have any of the intimate associations that

13. *Ruth surrounded by bamboo trees on her way to see Mr Dean.*

are privileged in the film and is therefore less emotionally charged. The structures of looking in the film are remarkable since there is an extreme close-up of Mr Dean's eyes, watching Sister Ruth from behind the trees as she enters his hut. This is important in creating a sense of suspense, because when she enters the hut we know that Mr Dean is watching: her apparent intimate reverie of being close to him is not what it seems.

When Mr Dean enters Ruth tells him that she has left the Order and that she loves him. He rebuffs her passionate declaration and offers to take her back to the palace. She accuses him of loving Clodagh, he declares that he doesn't love anyone and, as the tension between them mounts, she repeats Clodagh's name over and over and the screen gradually turns to red to replicate her intense emotional disturbance, anger and eventual fainting. When she collapses the screen darkens completely. Powell uses an extreme close-up of Ruth's eyes when she awakens, her brow beaded with sweat, to indicate her escalating disturbance and a sense of resolve, although at that time we do not know exactly what she has decided. She refuses Mr Dean's offer to accompany her back to the convent, kissing his hand as he helps her on with a coat. The sequence ends with a dissolve from a close-up of Mr Dean's face to Clodagh's as she waits for news of Sister Ruth. Powell often ends scenes with a dissolve. In this instance it represents empathy between Mr Dean and Clodagh: Ruth is a problem for both of them. It is as if he fully comprehends Clodagh's dilemma as she anxiously awaits news of Ruth. At the same time the potentially dangerous implications of Ruth's behaviour have been suggested, the humiliation to be experienced by someone who does not conform to the codes of behaviour expected of her, even though she has given up the Order. The cycle of complete psychological disturbance has begun, as a prelude to the 'musical sequence' when Ruth begins to stalk Clodagh, leading up to the climactic scene at the bell tower.

This sequence, probably the most celebrated in the film, takes place within a specific time-frame (it lasts nearly seven minutes but is supposed to take place over about fifteen). It begins early in the morning, as the dawn breaks, with Sister Clodagh watching for the missing Sister Ruth outside the convent, the implication being that she has waited up for news all night. The pink, mauve and dark grey colours for this shot form the dominant palette for the following scenes. This carefully constructed sequence takes place with dialogue only at the very beginning. Joseph Anthony brings Clodagh a glass of milk, telling her that

14. *Ruth about to attack Clodagh.*

it is 5.45 and that the people call this time 'the flowering of the snows'.
Ignoring this, Clodagh wearily tells him that she can be found in the
chapel. We then see the first of several shots that are clearly structured
from another point of view, that of Sister Ruth watching Clodagh from
further back as she goes to the chapel. An extreme close-up of Ruth's
eyes confirms this disturbing knowledge, her brow heavily beaded with
sweat, strands of lank, dishevelled hair hanging down. Her eyes are dark
and disturbed, setting the suspenseful mood for the next shots by cueing

15. *Ruth and Clodagh struggle at the bell tower.*

the viewer to expect danger. As Duncan Petrie points out: 'The dawn
sequence building up to the climax of the film as Clodagh is stalked
by Ruth is a *tour de force* of cinematic power, where the audience is
forced to share Ruth's POV as stalker.'[35] In the chapel the pink early
light is visible through the high windows, as Clodagh staggers forward
looking exhausted. The cloak she is wearing over her habit is less than

spotless. Her psychological state is clearly fragile as she collapses in despair. This deterioration of the nun in charge of the Order creates a further link between the two women: as Ruth's appearance has changed dramatically Clodagh is also physically marked by the recent crisis.

We see a door opening and again know that Ruth is watching Clodagh. This time we don't see her but hear a noise that alerts Clodagh to the possibility that she might not be alone. Ruth dashes up the stairs; Clodagh gets up, turning her head quickly to see who is there and again the camera takes the point of view of a dangerous voyeur from afar as we are not quite sure whether Clodagh has seen Ruth. Supported by ominous music and after building up the tension to this point, the mood relaxes a little when Clodagh remembers that it must be nearly six o'clock and therefore time for her to ring the bell. As duty momentarily distracts her from the immediate sense of fear, she walks out to the bell; the camera utilises the diffusing technique deployed by Jack Cardiff referred to in the previous chapter as it follows her. The effect creates a slightly unnerving, dreamlike mood as Clodagh walks alongside the outside wall of the palace, touching it with her hand to steady herself. As Clodagh starts to ring the bell we see Ruth emerge through the door, the same one we saw her open when we were first introduced to her at the beginning of the film. Her appearance is striking: her dress looks almost black, her face white, hair wet and lank. Staring resolutely towards the bell, she appears almost as a vampire, a creature from a horror film in pursuit of her victim (see illustration 14). The soundtrack's rising choral strains build in a crescendo, enhancing the mood of impending danger. The struggle between the two women begins as the editing and music quicken their pace simultaneously. Ruth pushes Clodagh over the ledge, but she does not fall to her death because she is hanging on to the bell rope. Suspense is heightened when the camera shows part of their fight by focusing on their feet, as Ruth tries to prevent Clodagh from scrambling back on to the ledge. Ruth tries to prise Clodagh's hands from the rope but falls over the ledge as Clodagh manages to struggle back up (see illustration 15). As Ruth falls we hear a scream and see a close-up of a horrified Clodagh looking over the precipice, her hand over her mouth and eyes wide open. Drums thud in the background as we see via a low-angle shot the bamboo trees below in the valley. The drums stop, birds fly upwards, presumably as Ruth falls through the trees to the ground.[36] In this dazzling sequence the 'problem' of Sister Ruth has been excised; both novel and film include this climactic event that finally convinces the Sisters that their mission is over.

Ruth's death is 'necessary' so that Clodagh can resume her life as a nun; it is intertwined with the recuperation of her faith at narrative closure. But the presentation of competing femininities – Clodagh's responsible, yet vulnerable behaviour pitted against Ruth's rebelliousness – has been a key dynamic. Arguably, the conflict between the two nuns is one of the most acute in the film and the camera's play with point of view is an effective mechanism of conveying this tension. Indeed, as we have seen, both Clodagh and Ruth survey each other's behaviour in a series of powerful looks between women. The intensity of their exchanges is compelling, for example in the powerful scene described earlier in which Ruth puts on lipstick in front of Clodagh. This completes the cycle of fascination that has been established between them, as Clodagh crumbles under the weight of her responsibilities with a sense of failure exacerbated by Ruth's melodramatic flight from the palace and her return, associated with stalking and demonic possession. These forces threaten to invade Clodagh's entire sense of self-worth and even her vocation. Ruth's death restores the order that her rebellion has disrupted and, by implication, Clodagh's ability to conform to the strictures established by the Order. As the nuns are leaving Mopu, Mr Dean asks Clodagh what she will do. She replies that she'll be sent to another convent, but not as Sister Superior, indicating that she has been humbled by her experience. But she also implies that she will continue her work as a nun in India – the imperial missionary spirit will prevail in spite of the contradictions and problems that *Black Narcissus* has so acutely exposed. The extent to which this sense of 'closure' is convincing will be discussed in the next section, in which it is argued that the novel provides a more resolute ending than the film.

A COLONIAL POINT OF VIEW?

As will already be apparent, point of view is structured in a complex way in *Black Narcissus*. The narrative would appear to be primarily concerned with Sister Clodagh's task of making a success of St Faith, dealing with her appointment as Sister in charge, privileging her memories by granting her four flashbacks and pitting her will against the challenges of Mopu, Mr Dean and Sister Ruth. In many ways it appears to be *her* story, yet it is clearly Mr Dean's authority, insight and point of view that are privileged. Even though the majority of literal point-of-view shots concern the nuns looking, observing one another and their environment, ironically, it is the main male character who dominates the narrative. Ella Shohat and Robert Stam have also noted this feature: 'While the narrative is largely focalized through the nuns, the textual norms are ultimately embodied by the British man.'[37] As Mr Dean predicts, the nuns leave before the rains break and have made no more impression on Mopu than the Order of Brothers who previously failed to make their mark. Mr Dean's critique of the ways in which they conduct their faith is also accorded sense and insight. His views articulate a form of pantheism (a doctrine that God is everything and everything is God; all Gods can be worshipped) and a liberal approach to Christianity, for example in the arguments he uses to persuade Clodagh to leave the Holy Man undisturbed.[38] When she says that she thinks he ought to be removed, Mr Dean points out that his presence is essential at Mopu, chiding her for her rigidity by asking, 'What would Christ have done?' Similarly, at Christmas, when the young General 'congratulates' Clodagh on the birth of Christ, she gently reproaches him for speaking too casually about Christ, after which Mr Dean reminds her that on the contrary, Christ should be 'very much a part of life', not some distant, formidable figure. In this way it is as if he is educating her to teach Christian beliefs in a way that is appropriate to the East. Mr Dean emerges therefore as being complicit with the idea that aspects of Christianity might be relevant in India, yet his suggestions regarding interpretation are rendered less dogmatic and more universally spiritual. As the novel explains, Mr Dean believed that 'In God's house it should be better to be poor than rich … in your Church, you seem to me as far removed from His teaching as any other business institution'.[39]

In visual terms, this position of authority is first suggested by his voiceover as Clodagh reads his letter describing Mopu at the beginning of the film: his is the first, dominant view we get of the place, even though, as we have seen, this is then displaced by images that do not necessarily connect with his voiceover narration. He is also given the last shot of the film, watching the nuns leave as the rains begin in a close-up that signifies his 'natural' position being in control of narrative, situation and environment. Also, in his mastery of most difficult situations – even when a desirous Sister Ruth arrives on his doorstep – he maintains an air of authority that accords with his dominant 'voice' throughout the film. While the young General wears sumptuous clothes and jewels, Mr Dean is dressed minimally in shorts and on one occasion without a shirt to emphasise his rugged, physical form of masculinity. Powell and Pressburger exaggerated Godden's descriptions of Mr Dean revealing his bare legs and generally appearing scantily clad by presenting him as the polar opposite to the young General, who is associated with the nuns and femininity: he works with them at the school, frequently changes his spectacular outfits to cause comment, does not expose his flesh and wears perfume. Even though the film is primarily about the concerns of women, femininity and sexuality, Mr Dean's positioning in this way arguably undermines the potential power of the 'hysterical' forces unleashed. Their function is to support the thesis he has proposed: that Mopu is no place for a nunnery.

Mr Dean's authority also represents a significant aspect of both the novel's and the film's stance on colonialism. It is this aspect that makes his overall authority particularly significant and more than a simple case of male dominance over a melodramatic narrative. His assumed constant presence in Mopu is perhaps an indication of Godden's (and Powell and Pressburger's) belief that some aspects of British involvement in India could be positive. The novel makes clear that the British do not rule Mopu directly: the land was leased to the General's father for 'experimental development' by the British government.[40] As the General's agent, Mr Dean occupies an intermediary role in the colonialist context, but at the same time the local people are accorded a degree of autonomy and are to some extent respected by him. His rejection of the missionary work invited by the General therefore acts as a critique of this type of British presence in India, proposing an interesting counter to a key element of colonialist activity. In 1939, when the novel was written, this anticipates the final years of colonial rule, with the British being 'in' India but not 'of it'. As Bagchi argues by drawing on the theoretical model proposed by Homi Bhabha, this scenario allows Mopu to become 'reinscribed as a site of hybridity' in the sense that its position as 'both inside and outside colonial and princely rule' frustrates and ultimately defeats the nuns' ability to enforce Western notions of superiority, civilisation and knowledge:

> The non-colonial/not-princely space is transformed into a site that is fraught with multivalences. On this site we witness a strange reversal; instead of the nuns resignifying the site of the 'House of Women' and the lives of the natives, the site and the people resignify not only the nuns' subjectivities but also their faith in the White Man's Burden.[41]

This reading would support the idea that *Black Narcissus* is a radical text, operating as a critique of colonialism. While it has been acknowledged by Priya Jaikumar that 'place' in the film acts as a key destabilising factor, especially in relation to other British imperial narratives, as I have stressed above, the structuring of point of view ultimately to privilege Mr Dean should also be taken into account when qualifying this argument.[42] After all, the vindication of Mr Dean's predictions can be seen to represent the triumph of one form of Western intervention over another. While he objects to the nuns' mission, he is not free from colonial attitudes in his one-dimensional view of the people of Mopu as children, his paternalist sense of responsibility over Kanchi and possibly sexual connection with her, and use of servants in his home.[43] In this and other respects his dominating presence is extremely significant, especially since he represents a class of English intermediary, an agent who has learned to survive and maintain a good life from the opportunities presented by the model of 'inside and outside' colonialist-princely regime at Mopu.

At the end of the novel Mr Dean is not present on the last morning, leaving us in the final pages with Clodagh and her thoughts. In the film we learn that Clodagh will probably be sent to another convent, but her renewed sense of purpose is much stronger in the book. The scene of which Jack Cardiff was very proud, but which was cut from the final print, is of Clodagh returning to Calcutta to see Reverend Mother. Powell describes it:

> The young nun is crying, as she confesses her failure to establish the new post and save Sister Ruth from her dreadful fate. The rain beats upon the window and the tears stream down her face as she confesses her failure and then raises her tear-stained face in disbelief as she hears the old Mother Superior say: 'Don't cry, my child. It is the first time I have been really satisfied with you'.[44]

The Criterion Collection DVD of *Black Narcissus* contains two black-and-white stills of this scene. They show Clodagh at Mother Superior's feet, in a tender pose, looking up and leaning on her. These contrast greatly with the scenes between the two nuns at the beginning of the film, the implication being that she is now truly humbled by her experience. In the book Clodagh does not go to Calcutta but receives a reply to a letter she wrote to Mother Dorothea, telling her about all the problems they encountered at Mopu. Mother Dorothea's letter praises her for her courage, pleased that she finds a 'new Clodagh, one whom I had long prayed to meet'. Clodagh also felt 'something strange' was happening to her, 'as if she were born again … a birth out of death'.[45] According to Cardiff the scene of Clodagh's return to Calcutta was cut because Powell considered the film's ending was stronger with the rain plopping on the leaves and then on Mr Dean's face.[46] In his autobiography Powell, however, regrets cutting the scene: 'I think we were bloody fools to cut it and substitute it for a highly romantic – or should I say High Romantic – shot of Mr Dean.'[47] Yet for the novel a clear indication that Clodagh has been spiritually strengthened by her experience is important: 'In these long days something strange was happening to Sister Clodagh. She thought it was as if she were born again; as if at the end of their time at Mopu had come the birth of a new Clodagh, a birth out of death.'[48] The novel also includes a character called Sister Adela, who replaces Sister Philippa and is appalled at the evidence of distraction from duty that has intruded into life at St Faith. After the dramatic events leading to the closure of the convent, she comments that 'we must look forward to trying again somewhere else', implying an unwavering faith in the missionary spirit.[49] The absence of both Sister Adela and Mother Dorothea's letter (or the equivalent scene shot by Cardiff) from the film arguably leaves a greater sense of ambivalence about Clodagh's future and, by implication, of British missions in India. It is in this sense that the film provides an apposite example of Homi Bhabha's conception of the 'third space', of the anticipation of a post-colonial perspective created out of the inherent ambivalences of colonial discourse.

In this way the film is able to suggest a complex stance on questions of colonialism, picking up the novel's threads but – perhaps unwittingly – pushing them further towards critique by providing compelling visual testimony to the processes of 'reinscription' and 'resignification' described by Bagchi.[50] While the supremacy of Mr Dean's perspective, and particularly his 'informal' approach to imperialism is endorsed, I have argued that the film none the less suggests that a complex, unresolved process is taking place in India on the eve of independence. Its cultural importance therefore exceeds its stature in the canon of Powell and Pressburger films. Yet the approach to adaptation was key in drawing out from Godden's novel the multiple layers of complexity that have been highlighted. As a source text the novel was crucial. As we have seen, many of the most riveting scenes were taken directly from its pages, including lines of dialogue. Yet the striking deployment of cinematic conventions creates significant differences between novel and film. The extreme close-ups used on several occasions of Sister Ruth's eyes convey visually the character's intensity, in particular her jealousy of and obsession with Sister Clodagh. Powell's decision to link scenes with dissolves instead of direct cuts enhances the sense of disturbing links between the past and the present that I have argued are so important for appreciating the film's troubling evocation of 'recognition lurking under the exotic'.[51] Used in conjunction with low-key lighting, Jack Cardiff's 'painterly' use of Technicolor is capable of conveying subtleties of mood that would have been impossible had a different cinematographic approach been deployed. Under his direction colour vividly captures the exoticism of Leonardslee's azaleas and rhododendrons, as well as the excessively splendid silks and jewels worn by the young General. On other occasions, as the analysis of the sequence when Sister Ruth 'stalks' Clodagh demonstrates, it is used in an expressionist way via the privileging of a pink, mauve and grey-black colour palette to create suspense. When the same colour palette is used for Calcutta at the beginning of the film it connotes order and regimentation; by the end of the film these same colours illustrate the extent to which order has completely broken down at St Faith. Colours therefore alter their meaning according to context. The precise, controlled vision of the East created by Alfred Junge similarly shifts meaning in curious ways. On some occasions it functions as the mysterious 'Other' of the Western imagination, while on others it is strangely familiar to the West, as in the vivid flashback when Clodagh's memory is visually linked by shots of the blue sky and blossoms at Mopu and the stunning landscape of Ireland that forms the backdrop to her own 'exotic' appearance in her former life.

In this and other respects *Black Narcissus* was a remarkable and controversial film. For Rumer Godden the novel had been a turning-point in her career. She had noticed an unknown nun's grave while on a picnic in Cherrapunji, an intriguing sight that triggered her idea for the novel twelve years later. Its success encouraged her to write more, to experiment with her craft and further communicate her fascination with India. Similarly for Powell and Pressburger, the film was an important stage in their creative development. It confirmed that a controlled studio environment was ideal for achieving the highly stylised, melodramatic effects that typified subsequent films such as *The Red Shoes*. For all its celebrated technical achievements *Black Narcissus* was, not, however an unreserved critical success. The following chapter demonstrates the extent to which contemporary commentary extended far beyond the usual arenas of film reception when the film's subject-matter, and mode of conveying the nuns' experiences, convinced many viewers that there was indeed 'something in the air that makes everything seem exaggerated'.

THREE
Reception

Black Narcissus was released in Britain on 26 May 1947. Some reviews were ambivalent, mainly because the film departed from the contemporary critical trend of privileging realism above more melodramatic forms. The unsettling representation of place appeared also to trouble some critics. The *Daily Telegraph* reviewer, for example, commented on 'the oddly uncomfortable air of a work which has never quite decided on its mood'.[1] These qualities came to be appreciated later, when the film acquired 'classic' status in the 1970s–1980s revival of interest in the films of Powell and Pressburger and more general appreciation of melodramatic forms, but at the time of release the film was not heralded as such. Arthur Vesselo, reviewing the film for *Sight and Sound*, described it as 'a disappointment, redeemed only in parts by its acting and photography'.[2] Writing in the *Observer*, C. A. Lejeune remarked that 'The colour is beautiful, imaginatively chosen, tactfully used and arranged, in scene after scene with the vision of a painter; so that the ravished eye carries the willing mind more than half way to satisfaction. This is just as well since the story ... is just a little too subtle for the producers' craft.'[3] The exhibitor-dominated periodicals were on the whole positive, demarking the film for 'discerning' patrons, wary of how it might be received by the majority of cinema-goers. The *Kinematograph Weekly* reviewer commented, for example, that 'There is, of course, more than a possibility that intelligent audiences, those who have the imagination to fill in story gaps, will find it stimulating, but its neglect of the heart is almost certain to prejudice its chances in tough industrial quarters.'[4] These comments are remarkable, especially since the film ends in such a spirit of high melodrama. The existence of 'story gaps' and expectations that audiences could only 'read' the film through its 'subtleties' actually implied a puzzled reception from critics regarding the subject-matter. The most frequent adjectives used in reviews were 'different', 'strange', 'unusual', 'daring', 'exotic', 'provocative', 'controversial', 'curious' and 'challenging', but while the film was generally marked as notable, praise tended to be centred on its distinguished technical qualities. The style that so unsettled its characters appeared to have had a similar effect on its reviewers. Despite these critical reservations, the film did well at the box-office.[5]

'CONDEMNED!': *BLACK NARCISSUS* IN THE USA

As an independent production company releasing its films through the Rank Organisation, the largest British film company at that time, The Archers benefited from Rank's link with the American company Universal, forged in the summer of 1945. Rank had previously released its films in the USA through United Artists, but the American distribution company had not handled the release of *The Life and Death of Colonel Blimp* at all well, with serious box-office consequences.[6] In 1946 Universal-International was formed to handle 'prestige' pictures, while the distribution company Eagle-Lion handled other films. Since several British films had been successful when targeted to metropolitan, 'niche' markets, it was likely that the film would do well in the USA, especially since *A Matter of Life and Death* (US title *Stairway to Heaven*) and *I Know Where I'm Going!* were popular, particularly in New York. Despite these internationalist aspirations, the British film industry was, however, entering into a volatile period, exacerbated by Britain's acute financial dependence on the USA since the end of the Second World War. A major crisis occurred, known as 'The Dalton Duty Crisis', in July–August 1947, when an attempt was made to curtail dollar remittances to the USA in respect of the high proportion of Hollywood's films shown on British screens. This controversy became popularly known as the 'Bogart or Bacon' debate, fuelled by rhetoric as deployed by politicians such as Robert Boothby in the House of Commons: 'If I am compelled to choose between Bogart and bacon I am bound to choose bacon at the present time.'[7] Also opting for bacon, Parliament sanctioned the imposition of a 75 per cent *ad valorem* duty on American film imports and a vengeful Hollywood retaliated by boycotting the British market: no new films were sent to Britain from August 1947 until June 1948, when a settlement was reached. Rank, and other large British film production companies, frantically tried to fill the gap created by the American boycott, but since the crisis had occurred at a time when the British film industry was not well prepared for a sharp increase in production, it did not result in a major revival of the industry and exacerbated the Rank Organisation's financial problems.[8] The bitterness caused by the Dalton Duty Crisis was not conducive to a positive reception for *Black Narcissus* in the USA, even if the religious issue had not prevailed.

Black Narcissus obtained a certificate from the British Board of Film Censors (BBFC) without any trouble, but in America its history was completely different.[9] The release of *Black Narcissus* in the USA was beset with controversy, providing an example of how in the short term, a British film could be adversely affected when its release was held up by the process of censorship. Several key sequences, including the flashbacks of Sister Clodagh's past life in Ireland, were excised from the American release print. As we have seen, these flashbacks are of fundamental importance to the film, their evocation of memory linking the past and present. When *Black Narcissus* was first released it was therefore available in different versions, a key fact that must be taken into account when attempting to understand its contemporary significance.

The cuts were the result of the work of the Catholic Legion of Decency (LOD) rather than the Production Code Administration (PCA), the body with primary responsibility for film censorship in the USA. Although it had no statutory authority, the PCA was a censorship organisation established by the film trade in 1934 to offset criticism of a perceived decline in moral standards on the screen. Headed by Joseph Breen, the PCA awarded films certificates, or 'seals' as they were popularly known, and the majority of cinemas owned by the major studios agreed not to show films without PCA approval.[10] American censorship was strict and Joseph Breen's office wielded a considerable degree of authority over which films, and in what form, were released; many had to be cut in order to receive a PCA certificate. The Breen office was not, however, the only organisation with control over film content. The LOD, formed in 1934, also censored films and worked in close collaboration with the PCA. Its collusion with and influence over the PCA reflects the power of Catholicism in many metropolitan centres all over the USA. A film's release could be boycotted and even prevented if the LOD disagreed with a PCA decision to issue it with a seal. As Gregory Black has commented: 'The Legion had a direct, overt effect on the content of Hollywood films; it also had a "chilling" effect on studio executives, producers, directors, and writers, who realized that certain subjects were either banned from the screen or could be presented only within a certain framework because of

Catholic opposition.'[11] British films seeking American exhibition also had to negotiate this system and were therefore constrained by the same sensitivities over the representation of particular subjects, notably religion, as were American films.

Operating alongside the PCA code, the Legion devised its own categorisation system in 1936 (A1 = unobjectionable for general patronage; A2 = unobjectionable for adults; B = objectionable in part and C, the rating given to *Black Narcissus* = condemned). In many cases, such as that of *Black Narcissus*, this rating system was utilised as an authoritative register of disapproval. The purview of the Legion extended beyond judgement over particular films to extensive comment on the affairs of the film industry. One of the key figures who colluded with the Catholic-dominated PCA and with the LOD was Martin Quigley, co-author of the original PCA code and a prominent Catholic film industry press baron. Producers who tried to challenge the Legion, for example David Selznick over *Duel in the Sun* in 1946–47, found no support from fellow producers and ended up having to comply with the Legion's insistence on cuts. The case of *Black Narcissus* came at a time when the LOD was therefore at the height of its power – so powerful that in this case it was able to challenge the judgement of the PCA itself. *Black Narcissus* was the first major film to cause controversy with the LOD since their protracted opposition during 1941–43 against another 'condemned' film, *The Outlaw*.[12]

The debate over the censorship of *Black Narcissus* can therefore be related to the LOD's influence over cinema and, in view of the film's setting and thematic preoccupations, to a wider context of East–West relations. On a broader level, the case provides an example of how censorship is representative of a convergence of systems of power and authority rather than the activity of a single organisation. In this way the interaction between different institutions can be seen to foster an overall context of constraint, revealing the many complex ideological preoccupations at stake in the process. It is clear that the existence of a framework of negotiation between the PCA, LOD and the film industry, contributed to the tenacity and longevity of the censorship system in the USA.

As early as April 1945 William Burnside of Eagle-Lion (at that time Rank's US distributor) sent a 'very rough draft' of *Black Narcissus* to Joseph Breen's office. A warning was given that it might cause offence in religious quarters; the story was considered to be risqué from the start.[13] Breen wrote:

While the story is not quite clear and concise, to us it has about it a flavor of sex sin in connection with certain of the nuns, which, in our judgment, is not good. We are apprehensive that any motion picture in which there would be even the slightest implication of sex sin or sexual longings or desires on the part of the women consecrated to religion, would give great offense to religious-minded folk in this country and might well call forth very vigorous and, possibly, violent protest from them.[14]

The whole idea that Sister Clodagh had become a nun after being disappointed in love was also considered to be 'highly questionable', likely to be distasteful to many people and, moreover, 'wound and offend them'.[15] Powell and Pressburger gave assurances that this would be avoided and further scripts were sent and revised, including some lines spoken by Mr Dean. Breen instructed: 'Please change the underlined word in Mr Dean's line, "I've come to mend a loose joint in *your* pipe." The plumbing must not refer to water closets or toilets. We question the further line "I swear to you, Sister, it's only the pipe I'm interested in" in order to avoid the sex inference which embarrasses the Sister.'[16] This type of intervention was typical of Breen's office since the PCA took the opportunity to work with producers on scripts, almost becoming collaborators on particular productions. Viewing this scene today the objections seem ridiculous, especially taking into account David Farrar's ironic delivery of the lines, which were not excised despite Breen's early objection.

In May Powell and Pressburger reassured Breen that they had revised the script with his comments in mind, and that they were more than satisfied with the results: 'We both feel sure that we shall have a production to be proud of and quite clear in its moral implications and power to do good.'[17] The PCA passed *Black Narcissus* in June 1947, with the proviso that a foreword should be added making it clear that the nuns were Anglo, as opposed to Roman, Catholic. Breen wrote the foreword: 'Throughout the world a group of faithful nuns of the order (fill in name) carry on the charitable work of the Church of England. Outside of the British Empire not much is known of their activities. Each year they are given the choice of renewing their vows as nuns. To them and to their work we dedicate this film.'[18] In Breen's opinion, the film was 'superb'; assured Father John McLafferty of the LOD, New York, that 'we need have no serious worry about this picture on any score'.[19] His previous concerns about Sister Clodagh's past love affair had clearly been forgotten at this point, Breen miscalculating that the foreword would placate Catholics. At the same time that the film was passed by the PCA it was banned by the Irish censor, Richard Hayes, on 12 June 1947 on the grounds that

> There is a sex atmosphere right through the picture which many will regard as a travesty of convent life. I fear that the picture will be misunderstood by large numbers in Ireland who will associate it with all the old caricatures of conventional orders. The Mother Superior ... is more reminiscent of a Hollywood star than of the head of a religious order.

On 25 June the film was, however, passed with undetermined cuts by the Appeals Board.[20] It is interesting that *Black Narcissus* was subject to a religious-inspired objection in Ireland at the same time as the American campaign was evolving.

The LOD had begun its protest in April 1946 when news of the film was picked up by the Archbishop of Calcutta from an item in the *Times of India*.[21] The LOD, with its powerful organisation all over the USA and with contacts in the UK, began an elaborate, highly orchestrated and effective campaign against the film's release as alarm spread in Catholic circles. The Archbishop wrote a letter to the editor of *The Sword of the Spirit* who forwarded it to Father John McLafferty, who in turn urged J. J. Campbell, J.P., of Glasgow, to communicate with Joseph Breen who at that time was visiting London. Ironically, the purpose of Breen's visit was to advise British producers about how to negotiate the American censorship system.[22] Father Patrick J. Masterson, a powerful figure in the LOD in New York, contacted Reverend Mother Leticia Gallardon in Kansas City, urging her to take legal action against the film because the name of the Order of which she was in charge was the same as the name used in *Black Narcissus*: the Servants of Mary.[23] All of this threatening correspondence was forwarded to John O'Connor, Vice-President of Universal-International, the film's US distributor, as an indication of the trouble that lay ahead if they persisted in releasing the film.

The LOD was highly influential in the Catholic press, and in July 1947 a damning review by Virginia S. Tomlinson was published in *The Tidings*, the Catholic weekly of the Los Angeles diocese.[24] Tomlinson described the film's portrayal of the nuns as 'hysterical, frustrated, neurotic, lovestarved and worldly'. She also wrote: 'It is a long time since the American public has been handed such a perverted specimen of bad taste, vicious inaccuracies and ludicrous improbabilities.' She also noted that in the version she had seen the foreword was printed only on the programmes. As Breen had anticipated – but not insisted on removing it – the scene that caused most offence was Sister Clodagh's flashback of her past life in Ireland and her love for Con. An appalled Virginia Tomlinson wrote: 'Sister Clodagh ... kneeling at the altar, her mind intent – not on prayer – but ... going over a love-scene of her own youth'. This proved to be a most controversial sequence, the excision of which had profound consequences for the film. Predictably, the scenes of Sister Ruth putting on red lipstick were severely criticised by the Catholics as a representation of a nun who demonstrated the twin evils of a rebellious attitude coupled with sexual desire. Tomlinson's conclusion was damning:

> No intelligent adult, viewing this picture, will fail to admit that it is nothing but a stupid attempt at the sensational ... Mr Rank is standing on very shaky ground. Whether such a picture portrays Catholic nuns or Protestant nuns, he is attacking the known sanctity of a group of women whose lives are (as he says) dedicated to sacrifice and work and who stand for all that is holy and above reproach in a rocking world.

Tomlinson's review had serious consequences. Father Patrick J. Masterson sent it to Universal-International and informed *The Tidings* that: 'You may be sure that the boys at Universal saw it and paused. We're trying to add some more fuel to the flame, in the hope of getting Mr Rank to bring his picture back to England and perhaps dump it on the way over.'[25] The review also persuaded Martin Quigley to join in the crusade against the film's release. He disseminated it widely, which encouraged the writing of the 'Notre Dame letter', a key communication in the controversy. This was written by a committee appointed by the Sisters' Vocation Institute, which met at Notre Dame University to discuss how to increase dwindling recruitment to the various Sisterhoods. The letter, written in July 1947, protested against the film, declaring that the foreword was inadequate and that the film 'ridiculed all religion'.[26] It was felt that the average cinema-goer would not distinguish between Anglican and Roman Catholic nuns. The 'modern world' was blamed for the shortage of Sisters, a situation that would not be helped by a film like *Black Narcissus*, which depicted the nuns as unhappy, or at least not entirely content, with their choice. It warned of the dangers of allowing the film to be taken as a representative account of the work of nuns, drawing attention to their role in the Second World War and as 'educators' of local people abroad:

To imply that this isolated series of incidents is a typical instance of what goes on in convents and of what happens when Sisters are sent by their vow of obedience, freely made, to the foreign missions, would be diametrically opposed, for example, to the first-hand observation and experience of innumerable G.I.s, many of whom were rescued by natives Christianized [*sic*] by foreign mission nuns and priests, and nursed, helped, cheered, comforted and edified by the nuns themselves.

The strident letter was sent to J. Arthur Rank, Nate Blumberg (President of Universal-International), Eric Johnston (President of the Motion Picture Association of America) and to Joseph Breen's office. Breen's secretary was sent a copy by a Catholic friend who sent an accompanying note: 'All we Catholics should gang up on this picture – and with Mr Breen's help see that the stinky thing is stopped. I can't see how it got past your office – if it has. Anyway, we ought to let Rank keep his "rank" pictures and take them back to England.'[27] As a result of this protest the foreword to the film was changed, this time emphasising that the *Anglican* nuns were from 'Protestant Orders', renewing their vows annually.[28] As it turned out, Protestant groups did not object to the film.[29]

In the meantime, Universal went ahead with previewing the film. Rank attended the glittering Anglo-American première at the Carthay Circle Theatre, Los Angeles, on 7 July 1947, a significant event in his campaign to publicise Anglo-American co-operation. The event was reported widely in the press, the *Citizen News* claiming that: 'This initial showing of *Black Narcissus* at the Carthay Circle brought out what was probably the largest turnout of stars and top executives ever assembled at a Hollywood preview or première.'[30] Among the guests were Joan Bennett, Ingrid Bergman, Rosalind Russell, Norma Shearer, Shirley Temple and Phyllis Calvert.[31] It was definitely staged as an event designed to cement stronger Anglo-American relations even though the Dalton Duty crisis meant that impending conflicts were never far from the surface.

Prominent members of the LOD were invited to a special screening of the film in August, after which they nevertheless proclaimed it to be a 'condemned' picture (out of thirteen Fathers, eight gave it a 'C' rating, the rest recommending A2, unobjectionable for adults). Some reviewers objected to the film's 'Freudian' implications.[32] The term Freudian was used in a pejorative sense, referring to the film's portrayal of women who are in danger of failing to control their emotions and of rebelling against authority, particularly their 'problem' with their commitment, which is explained in terms of them being frustrated in love rather than dedicating their lives to Christianity. Others objected to its images of the 'pagan' East as seductive, offering a more attractive environment than the West. John O'Connor (not to be confused with the executive at Universal with the same name), a member of the International Federation of Catholic Alumnae's Motion Picture Department and of the official reviewing group of the LOD, articulated this position in an extensive document appended to his report:

> The symbolism of the convent-school-dispensary succumbing to the East, with the typical vague 'holy man', the mystical mountains, the primitive drums etc., all seemed vaguely reminiscent of the modern English authors who have wet their toes in the field of Oriental philosophy as has [*sic*] Huxley and Maugham and others. It seems to this reviewer that *Black Narcissus* may well set a pattern that is not compatible with the traditions of Christianity ... the beautiful setting, plus the technicolor shots of the country north of Darjeeling, will only attract the average theatre-goer to listen even more. My point is this: the West succumbs to the East in this film ... As we know from the Eastern influence in English Literature ... it is a mysticism that does away with personality, discrimination, definition, and presents as the ultimate of life, *nirvana*, a state in which the individual reverts to the primal flux of things ... I regard the message as a symbol.[33]

This review clearly points to the seductiveness of 'place' referred to earlier, and of the anxiety caused by the film's suggestion that the East might provide an attractive, mystical alternative to Christianity. It is almost as if the film is being interpreted as an exercise in propaganda for the East and, in this instance, as a disturbing text for those concerned to preserve the sanctity and imperialising function of missionary groups in India.

Hedda Hopper publicised the controversy and news spread fast of the Legion's ban.[34] In August Masterson met with representatives from Universal and Rank to explain the Legion's position fully. At that stage they were clearly pressing for an outright ban, since the point was made that editing, cutting or the addition of a prologue would not make the film suitable since its theme was fundamentally objectionable. Universal-International arranged some high-profile preview screenings in New York and Los Angeles, but wider distribution was prevented by protests and lobbying by the LOD. When the film opened in Los Angeles and the LOD intensified its campaign, bookings elsewhere were cancelled.[35] This furore was extremely bad timing for Rank, who was in the midst of the 'Dalton Duty crisis'. This was potentially disastrous for Rank's campaign to obtain more extensive and effective distribution of British films in the USA, as Anglo-American film relations grew very bitter. Rank was unable to withdraw the film as the Legion had requested because of commitments to Powell and Pressburger and to Universal. Since both Rank and Universal were both well-known and reputable companies their contract did not contain a clause whereby the distributor had the right after screening to distribute a picture or not. There was thus no 'escape clause' to protect the distributor against action taken by pressure groups such as the LOD; the company had no alternative but to show the film if Rank so wished.[36] The Legion's campaign continued, but by September Powell, Pressburger and Universal were forced to consider cutting the film. It seemed that the Legion's exhortations to the cinema chains not to show the film were not entirely successful. Fox West Coast Theatres decided to show *Black Narcissus* regardless, in part influenced by the fact that its notoriety by then *increased* its chances of attracting audiences.[37] Also, it became clear that although many enthusiastically endorsed the Legion's ban not all Catholics shared this condemnatory view.[38] Yet as September progressed there is evidence that because of the Legion's action screenings were cancelled in Detroit, Columbia and Memphis.[39] A compromise was reached when the decision was taken to cut the film so that the Legion might withdraw the controversial 'C' rating and Rank, Universal, Powell and Pressburger might make some profit out of this ill-fated project.

Since there was no opportunity to reshoot parts of the film the only solution was editing.[40] The cuts, ten in all, were suggested by Martin Quigley and reduced the film by 900 feet in total. These cuts included suggestive dialogue, such as Mr Dean saying to Sister Clodagh, 'I don't suppose you would want to talk to me on anything else', and to Sister Briony, 'You will be doing me a great favour when you educate the local girls.' Sister Clodagh's flashbacks of Ireland were cut as well as close-ups of Sister Ruth putting on lipstick and stockings, and parts of Sister Ruth's scenes with Mr Dean when she has escaped from the convent of St Faith. The explanatory foreword was further developed: 'A group of Protestant nuns in mysterious India find adventure, sacrifice and tragedy.' The 'C' ban was thus removed and *Black Narcissus* finally released with an A2 LOD rating. As discussed earlier, the scene in which Clodagh confesses her past life and present troubles to Mr Dean was not removed, placing the focus of the Legion's attention on visual representations of the past rather than on the information that Clodagh had had a failed love affair before she joined the Order.[41]

News of the cuts reached the press. The *New York Times* published a letter by a man who had seen the film in the summer of 1947 at a preview screening in New York and was dismayed to see the cut version later, claiming that the film was deprived 'of much of its impact and logic'.[42] By contrast, John O'Connor of Universal claimed that the editing had been done under the supervision of Emeric Pressburger, who considered the changes to be 'fair, reasonable and just', although a telegram Powell sent to Pressburger in November 1947 implies that Powell wasn't altogether happy with the cuts.[43] The contradictory nature of aspects of the LOD's criticisms and the frustration of their moral crusade in practice was made clear by William K. Everson in his notes for a Museum of Modern Art retrospective in 1980. Everson pointed out that one of the cuts had exactly the opposite effect of what was intended. Mr Dean's reprimand (he says: 'You can forget about it') of Sister Ruth when she attempts to seduce him was removed from the sequence. This resulted in the insinuation that the seduction had taken place and triggered Sister Ruth's subsequent madness.[44]

American reviews varied between *Variety*'s quip that it was '*Brief Encounter* in the Himalayas ... a story of sex-starved nuns and a man', and *American Cinematographer*'s high praise for the film's art direction, costume design and Technicolor cinematography by Jack Cardiff. The article by Herb Lightman in *American Cinematographer* remains an excellent source of technical information on the film and an extremely useful contemporary account of its innovatory qualities.[45] The *New York Times* reviewer commented: 'It is, of course, recognised by now that the English have been far more successful in using the chromatic process than our Hollywood experts.'[46] Cardiff's use of Technicolor was the most consistently praised aspect of the film in terms of contemporary commentary. The Anglophile National Board of Review selected the film as 'exceptional' in its magazine, reviewer John B. Turner commenting that 'never before in this reviewer's memory has Technicolor been so breathtakingly composed and filmed'.[47] One review, however, claimed that excellence in this area acted as an unfortunate distraction from the imperatives of good storytelling: 'Perhaps the directors were so bemused by Technicolor that they thought the lovely tints of the continuity would make the average spectator disregard the episodic nature of a work which should have stayed between the covers of a book.'[48] In a similarly critical mode, *Time* magazine labelled the film 'a striking example of bad art', while the *Citizen News* found it 'woefully weak in its plot ingredients' despite its 'challenging photoplay, daring story text, magnificent sets, costumes and color photography'.[49] The *New York Times* described it as a 'curiously fascinating psychological study', while the reviewer for *Time* magazine was concerned about the East not being portrayed as strange enough: 'Lovely as some of the Technicolor photographs are, they bring little of the strangeness to the audience's eyes', implying that portrayal of the East demanded an even more extreme realisation.[50] This is an interesting comment in view of the film's 'blurring' of East and West, since the reviewer is seeking a clearer demarcation, which could be read as a desire for a strictly binarist, Orientalist perspective. As we have seen, *Black Narcissus* serves up no such easy demarcation, which is one of the reasons it caused so much controversy. Most reviewers drew attention to the censorship controversy, which may have contributed to its notoriety on first release. Whatever the aesthetic and ideological consequences of the cuts, the film nevertheless made profits in America.[51] Ironically, it was American director Martin Scorsese, a Catholic, who resuscitated Powell and Pressburger's reputation in the 1980s and who contributed enthusiastic and admiring commentary to Criterion's DVD of *Black Narcissus*.

The case of *Black Narcissus* generated a vast bulk of documents that raise interesting questions about the consequences of American censorship. The religious issue predominated, but it also had wider implications. Participants in the controversy were not only concerned about the portrayal of the nuns, they were also uncomfortable with the film's vision of the East as seductive and enchanting. It is clear from the documents that the East–West dichotomy was one of the themes that commentators drew out. As already observed, in many ways *Black Narcissus* can be read as a film that implicitly references the decline of the British Empire. Just as the sisters are forced to withdraw from their 'civilising mission', the British had withdrawn from India (India Independence Act, July 1947). As bearers of Western influence the women in *Black Narcissus* fail to offer the East a sustained alternative to sensibilities which the film privileges as seductive. The post-war world was rapidly becoming a decolonised one, with the USA assuming an ever-increasing economic and political role, displaying many of the imperialist assumptions formerly held by the British Empire.

It seems that the controversy over *Black Narcissus* was not therefore simply confined to the objections of the Catholic Church. The film was certainly considered to be an attack on the Church, the issue that exercised most critics. However, as we have seen, it was also viewed as an attack on Western civilization. Virginia S. Tomlinson's review explicitly says that '[Rank] is attacking the known sanctity of a group of women whose lives are (as he says) dedicated to sacrifice and work and who stand for all that is holy and above reproach in a rocking world.' Religion thus stands in for stability, Western civilization, stasis, 'tamed' and sacrificial femininity. What we know and trust must not be seen to be under threat. Its defeat in *Black Narcissus* by powerful 'rocking' forces of sexuality, desire, nature, beauty and freedom appeared at a significant juncture in East–West relations when political divisions were being established (and re-established) after the Second World War. With hindsight, it is therefore ironic and intriguing to observe that the American print cuts out the scenes which blur a rigid East–West divide at a time when, as Said acknowledges, the USA was adopting the Orientalist mantle in the East.[52] Sisters Ruth, Clodagh and Philippa were looking outwards, beyond their immediate responsibilities, their memories perhaps contributed to the film's suggestion of the existence of an alternative space, a convergence between a remembered past and a more challenging future where strict divisions between East and West are no longer operable. By excising the flashbacks, the Legion of Decency therefore unwittingly punished the nuns and the film for presenting such an unsettling end-of-Empire fiction: in short, for daring to 'see too far'.

FOUR
Revival and Appropriation

Black Narcissus played an important part in the resuscitation of Powell and Pressburger's reputations as significant British film-makers. Martin Scorsese's enthusiasm for the film was a key element in this trend, as were the National Film Theatre's screenings of The Archers' work in the 1970s, organised by Kevin Gough-Yates (1971) and Ian Christie (1978). Restored prints, including *Black Narcissus*, rekindled interest in films that were connected with the 'lost continent' of British cinema, bringing to the surface traditions that the privileging of realism in critical writing had repressed. As Julian Petley observed: 'Powell explores a very different dimension of "Englishness" that is almost diametrically opposed to the cold, hard empiricism which lies at the cultural root of the realist aesthetic: Powell's ancestors are not Mill, Locke and Hume but Romanticism and the Gothic.'[1] The Gothic elements of *Black Narcissus* are particularly striking: the fantastical setting and haunting of Sister Clodagh by Ruth with her startling, demonic appearance. In the 1970s the critical climate was more receptive to films that did not fit into the realist canon and Powell and Pressburger's work came to be valued for its auteurism, affinity with European cinema and 'overflow' of emotion and mysticism.

The years following *The Red Shoes* (1948) were difficult, as Ian Christie commented: 'Few of those who came to know Powell during his later years of recognition ever realised how many disappointments and rebuffs he had suffered, the price he paid for espousing art and eschewing compromise.'[2] In the 1950s Powell and Pressburger produced several films, but these were less successful with critics and at the box-office, including *The Tales of Hoffmann* (1951) and *Oh Rosalinda!!* (1955); both films have since been appreciated as daring and experimental. But at the time it became increasingly difficult to get their films funded. Their last collaboration was a wartime drama, *Ill Met by Moonlight* (1956). Powell continued to work as a director, his most controversial post-Pressburger film being *Peeping Tom* (1959), which many contemporary critics found abhorrent for its portrayal of a serial killer. The film was later heralded as a key film in the evolution of the horror genre. Pressburger continued to write screenplays and novels, but undoubtedly his best work was with Powell. Each reinforced the other's strengths and, despite disagreements, readily acknowledged their mutual interdependence.

In the USA Powell and Pressburger's films were championed by art film enthusiasts and subsequently by Martin Scorsese and Francis Ford Coppola, directors who declared them to be decisive influences on their own work. In recognition of this Powell was invited to Hollywood in 1981 as director in residence in Coppola's Zeotrope studio. Not only was there evidence of a considerable critical re-engagement with Powell and Pressburger's films, but also there were two notable appropriations of footage from *Black Narcissus* in films made by lesbian/feminist directors in the 1980s and 1990s. Their films' usage of *Black Narcissus* will be the focus of this chapter, as well as the short film *Remembering Sister Ruth* (1997). These examples demonstrate an enduring fascination with *Black Narcissus* as a narrative that can be transposed into different contexts and modes of film-making.

DAMNED IF YOU DON'T (1987)

American avant-garde film-maker Su Friedrich was the first to use aspects of *Black Narcissus* as an inspiration for *Damned if You Don't*, a film about sexual repression, Catholicism and desire.[3] The film follows two women, a nun (Peggy Healey) and an artist (Ela Troyana), interweaving their growing attraction for one another with strands discussed below, and culminating in their eventual sexual union. Several intertexts support this layer of primary narrative: *Black Narcissus*; passages adapted from Judith Brown's book *Immodest Acts: The Life of a Lesbian Nun in Italy*, based on the case of Sister Benedetta Carlini, Abbess of a convent who from 1619–23 was investigated for alleged 'misconduct' and then imprisoned for thirty-five years; the recollections of women about their experiences of being taught in Catholic schools and recurrent imagery including sea creatures in a tank, a snake that curls through water and a swan filmed from behind park railings. I will consider the relation between *Black Narcissus* and these other elements, and assess their importance for *Damned if You Don't* as an avant-garde work that has appropriated a popular film in a highly unusual manner.

Friedrich filmed a television broadcast of *Black Narcissus* and used this downgraded copy in her black-and-white film, complete with roll bars that descend down the screen over the main images in a manner that is jarring to viewers used to seeing the film in its pristine, original format. While this might seem to be a somewhat perverse appropriation of a film renowned for its cinematographic precision and stunning colour photography, Friedrich decided that this particular rendition of *Black Narcissus* was perfect for what she wanted to do in *Damned if You Don't*. As she explained to Scott Macdonald: 'The way I frame the imagery, very close, is to me a way of appreciating the drama of the film ... it was fun to pare *Black Narcissus* down to the bone, to string the exciting moments together and really focus on the sexual hysteria at the core of the film.'[4] Rather than remove the roll bars or shoot the televised film broadcast again Friedrich decided to keep them, concluding that they added texture to the film in an unexpected way: 'It became really interesting to edit for the rhythm of the gestures within the shot, combined with the rhythm of the roll bars, combined with the cadence of speech at the moment.'[5] Indeed, this approach enhances the film's key dramatic moments, rendering the imagery rather dreamlike, which is in keeping with an association between *Damned if You Don't* and the avant-garde psychodramas identified by P. Adams Sitney as 'visionary' films.[6] The reference to rhythm and cadence also invites similarities between avant-garde appropriation and Powell's own ambitions for the 'musical film' that, as we have seen, are such an important element in *Black Narcissus*. From this perspective *Black Narcissus* is removed from its preferred viewing context, becoming instead a commentary on the complex strands that are contained within *Damned if You Don't*. In any case, it is assumed that the audience is probably not familiar with *Black Narcissus* (described by one reviewer of Friedrich's film as 'a stylish old potboiler'), so the images of the film as presented would probably not have appeared to be a travesty to the majority of viewers.

For all its serious meditation on religion, sexual attraction and emotional conflict, *Damned if You Don't* is representative of a phase of feminist film-making that had begun to reconnect with questions of pleasure. As Friedrich explains: 'I wanted to make something that I (and viewers) would enjoy. But I don't think I set out to contradict any other person's film or any other kind of filmmaking. It's true that when I go to films that are determined *not* to provide traditional pleasure, I end up being really frustrated or bored or angry.'[7] Consequently much of the voiceover commentary is inflected with a vital sense of humour, often counterpointed with images of a more 'serious' nature (and vice-versa). It can be compared with other feminist films that included explicit references to well-known films such as Sally Potter's *Thriller* (1979) that drew on Hitchcock's *Psycho* (1960) in order to deconstruct classical narrative cinema and in the process comment on the representation of women in art and the media.[8] Rather than completely reject the accustomed pleasures to be found in mainstream cinema, feminist film-makers such as Friedrich and Potter therefore appropriated popular representations as a means of reinforcing their work.

Damned if You Don't opens with the artist watching *Black Narcissus* on television, and Friedrich selects key scenes to illustrate the narrative that is summarised for us in voiceover (Martina Siebert). In this summary it is reduced to somewhat crude, yet astute, deductions regarding the main plot elements of *Black Narcissus*. Sister Clodagh is called 'the good nun', Sister Ruth 'the bad nun' and Mr Dean is highlighted as a disturbing presence. Over the relevant scenes we hear explanatory commentary, for example:

> After the Christmas service, the good nun explains to Mr Dean that he's drunk. 'If you have a spark of decency left in you, you won't come near us again!' He goes off singing 'I won't be a nun, no I shall not be a nun, for I am so fond of pleasure, I cannot be a nun.'
>
> (At this point the narrator and film-maker attempt to sing Dean's lines, introducing a humorous element.)
>
> The bad nun has begun to agree with him, so the good nun calls her in for a chat. They discuss whether a fondness for pleasure might preclude being a nun. Suddenly, the bad nun dispenses with theory and accuses the good nun of wanting Mr Dean herself. Feigning coolness, she dismisses the bad nun and tries working until she's too tired to think of anything else.
>
> And now, another crisis: a baby dies while under their care and the nuns' lives seem to be in danger:
>
> Call Mr Dean![9]

The effect of seeing the downgraded scenes combined with this sparse commentary is interesting. The rather humorous delivery of the voiceover brings out the melodrama and 'hysteria' of *Black Narcissus*. The curious projection of the television images draws attention to the use of close-ups in particularly intense scenes (in a few shots Friedrich enhances the close-ups by bringing us closer to the images with her own camera), emphasising the film's variations of texture and bringing out the conflict between Sisters Clodagh and Ruth. One detail is emphasised: the tapestry work Clodagh does when she is trying (as indicated at the end of the extract above) to distract herself from the problems at Mopu, Sister Ruth and the invasion of her consciousness by past memories. We see another tapestry later when the nun of *Damned if You Don't* is stitching a tapestry of Jesus, filling in the lips. This acts as a prelude to her own sensual encounter with the artist at the end of the film. It also creates a link between Clodagh's attempts to banish 'difficult' thoughts and feelings, and the anxiety caused by experiencing sexual attraction that is highlighted with reference to the nun of *Damned if You Don't*. There is a similar connection as the narrative of the nun and artist (who live on the same street) — their occasional encounters and curious glances — mirrors the structures of fascination and looking that occur in *Black Narcissus* between Clodagh and Ruth, particularly towards the end of the film. Friedrich wanted to covey the difficulties around sexual attraction, particularly in relation to Catholicism where, in the case of nuns consecrated to God, a conflict emerges between the sanctioned love associated with serving the world and God, and sexual love, which for these women is forbidden.

This theme connects with the other intertexts in that the story of Sister Benedetta, based on ecclesiastical papers discovered in the State Archive of Florence, reveals an extraordinary amount of detail about lesbian passion in the seventeenth century. *Damned if You Don't* quotes passages on the case from the testimony of Sister Crivelli who testified against Benedetta even though she was clearly her lover. Similarly, the recollections (in voiceover) of women who were taught by nuns at school are concerned with conveying a sense that despite their position and religion, the nuns did not flinch from discussion of sex with their pupils and frequently became objects of obsession in themselves: 'Oh, I remember this one, Sister Carol, oh, she didn't just go by "Sister", you just called her Carol. She was the head of the drama department and senior year I was in "Godspell", and oh, she was wonderful ... God, I used to get all these crushes on these nuns, I can't believe it!'[10] The film therefore juxtaposes repression with letting go, as the nun gradually capitulates to her desires in a way that was impossible for the Sisters in *Black Narcissus*. The recurrent imagery of the snake juxtaposed with the imprisoned swan also conveys this tension, as the two women represented by these symbols could not be more different at the beginning of the film. But even if the nun is eventually allowed to experience sexual pleasure at the end of *Damned if You Don't* the mingling of texts has suggested that this may not necessarily be the start of a new, untroubled life. At one point in the film, for example, Friedrich accompanies the voiceover recounting details from Sister Crivelli's testimony with visuals of nuns going about their everyday lives, walking around normally. This discordant aural-visual strategy conveys something of the emotional complexities of consecrating your life to the Church, since the coupling of Crivelli's damning testimony with scenes of everyday life on a New York street suggest the extent to which darker secrets are often repressed underneath a veneer of 'normality', all the more so when that 'normality' is never questioned. Again, there is perhaps a useful link to *Black Narcissus*, particularly in the Legion of Decency's crude attempts to 'police' the text via censorship. As we have seen, members of the Legion were profoundly disturbed by implications that the nuns might deviate from their calling and that they were capable of sensuous desires, irreverent, distracting thoughts and feelings. *Damned if You Don't* takes this cue from *Black Narcissus* and accentuates all of these in a way that the Legion, had it still existed, would have found even more abhorrent.[11]

A BIT OF SCARLET (1996)

Andrea Weiss made a film in 1996 that consisted of a selection of extracts from British films that either directly include gay and lesbian subject-matter, allude to it via camp or which can be read 'oppositionally' in terms of elevating gay/lesbian sub-texts. Groups of extracts were punctuated by actor Ian McKellen's witty introductions in voiceover, drawing attention to obvious cinematic stereotypes and themes of gay and lesbian experience that have been broached in British films. *Black Narcissus* was included in the selection. Weiss re-edited the sequence when Sister Clodagh discovers Ruth wearing a red dress. Realising that she is disturbed, Clodagh watches over Ruth as she puts on red lipstick. As argued in the previous chapter, this 'transformation' scene is remarkable for its visual intensity, editing, lighting and colour. It comes at a key point in the narrative just after Clodagh has discovered that Ruth has not renewed her vows and therefore left the Order. In *Black Narcissus* Easdale's music heightens the mood of suspense and shock around Ruth's physical transformation. Weiss did not use this musical track, replacing Easdale's low drum-beat punctuated with choral accompaniment with a jauntier, more romantic piano theme. Weiss's version cuts out the dialogue completely, using the original shots but omitting the ones where the actresses are clearly speaking, to create a powerful sequence that has the appearance of being about lesbian desire and seduction, emphasising the powerful series of looks between the two women in the original film. Weiss explains:

> What I wanted to do in *A Bit of Scarlet* is elevate the subtext, both to examine latent attitudes toward homosexuality in British cinema and also to see what happened when I actually put on the screen what gay/lesbian spectators 'see' when they/we try to hijack mainstream images. I loved the tension and sheer intensity in that scene, which could be read in a variety of ways.[12]

By excluding the dialogue the intimation of conflict between the women becomes more sexualised, especially since there is little overt context for the tension obviously building up between them. Clodagh's shocked expression, shot in close-up, on hearing Ruth's conviction that they want to silence her, is transformed into an expression that instead denotes fear of being presented with temptation. To reinforce this impression Weiss cuts out particular shots to intensify the dynamic between the desirous woman and repressed nun. When, for example, Ruth joins Clodagh at the table, sits down and picks up her mirror and lipstick, Weiss deletes the shot when Ruth begins to apply the lipstick. Instead, Weiss cuts straight to the reaction shot of Clodagh looking horrified, and then to the extreme close-up of Ruth putting on the lipstick, with the camera panning up to her eyes as they slowly fixate on Clodagh. This accelerates the impact of the following two shots in which Ruth and Clodagh's gestures are linked: Ruth closes her hand-mirror and Clodagh opens her Bible, as if she is trying extremely hard to resist Ruth's advances. In this way the sequence has been given a new meaning; the sub-textual interpretation Weiss wished to foreground has well and truly come out.

REMEMBERING SISTER RUTH (1997)

In 1997 Malcolm Venville directed a ten-minute film called *Remembering Sister Ruth*, broadcast on BBC2's *10 x 10* series. Kathleen Byron, filmed in black-and-white, was the focus of this meditation on her most famous acting part. Her recollections of working with Michael Powell and her conception of the role of Sister Ruth are intercut with striking colour scenes from *Black Narcissus*. The film opens with an extract from Michael Powell's autobiography: 'I have always had a special respect for Kathleen ever since she pulled a gun on me. A naked woman and a loaded gun are persuasive objects.'[13] This is a typical Powell recollection, full of mischievous egotism. Straight away Byron questions its authenticity, saying, 'If I wanted to attack somebody with a gun I wouldn't bother to take my clothes off!'[14] This introduces a key theme integral to *Remembering Sister Ruth*: revisionism. Byron provides many correctives to some of the myths that have grown up around Powell and *Black Narcissus*. She highlights her own contribution to the memorable screen performance of Ruth, citing an instance when she successfully defied Powell in achieving her conception of how Ruth would behave when she goes to see Mr Dean after she has escaped from the convent. Byron confirms that in the scene where Ruth goes to Mr Dean's place in the valley it was her idea to have her walk around the room looking longingly and lovingly at his possessions. This internal reverie is a key moment in the film, providing a brief sense of calm and the illusion that Ruth has 'come home'; she is momentarily at peace. This invites a refreshing re-evaluation of the key contributions made by actors and actresses to The Archers' films. In a desire to herald Powell and Pressburger as *auteurs* the work of their many significant collaborators tended to be overlooked by many critics. In *Remembering Sister Ruth* Byron speaks of conflicts with Powell over her portrayal of Ruth: he wanted the nun to be very 'mad', whereas she was determined to make it clear to audiences that as far as Ruth was concerned she was absolutely sane. Their disagreement had already been indicated in an interview in 1990 when she stressed the importance of reining in Ruth's 'madness':

> I thought she was quite sane really, just doing a lot of thinking inwards. I think she *is* a bit touched by the time she takes off the habit and gets into the red dress to visit Mr Dean in the bungalow. She's planning her escape. I think that's the beginning of the real switch to madness, which could have been avoided if he had been at all sympathetic, but he just sent her back.[15]

This insistence on the internal consistencies of Ruth's persona and predicament (she falls in love and therefore resolves to leave the Order) arguably prevented the character from becoming completely ridiculous. It also emphasised the important link with Clodagh who, as I have argued in Chapter Two, is uncomfortably compared (even similar) to Ruth on many occasions.

Ruth therefore emerges very much as Kathleen Byron's conception, one that was so striking it dominated her career for years afterwards. In *Remembering Sister Ruth* she speaks of her appearances in over forty films, yet she is still remembered as 'the mad nun'. A sense of poignancy is conveyed when we see Byron riding on the top of a double-decker bus. Her journey ends with a shot taken from inside the moving bus looking out of the window to the pavement below, aligning our point of view with that of Byron. We see a nun walking along in a white habit, her fleeting appearance almost ghostly. In shots such as this, and the actual ones from *Black Narcissus*, we are reminded of the film's compelling visual qualities as well as some of Ruth's most memorable lines. This scene also resonates with Rumer Godden's own experience of being surprised by seeing advertisements for her novel while riding on a London bus.[16] After the bus ride we see Byron doing a reading, emphasising the fact that she is still a working actress, and then at home, sitting down looking at reviews and posters of *Black Narcissus*. By filming Byron in black-and-white the contrasting shots from the film are made to appear more vivid, more exciting than the actress's everyday life today. Sister Ruth is still with her, even though she played the part fifty years earlier. The final credits are accompanied by the vision of the nun in white and the sound of the wind, as if to remind us of the power of *Black Narcissus* to invade our consciousness like the incessant wind blowing at Mopu.

All three films therefore draw on *Black Narcissus* in different and distinctive ways. While Friedrich's is perhaps the most unusual appropriation in that it actually changes the conventional mode of viewing the film, *Damned if You Don't* nevertheless conveys the melodramatic appeal and visual intensity of *Black Narcissus*. Weiss and Venville also highlight these elements for their own particular 'takes' on Sister Ruth. But Friedrich's film is much longer (forty-two minutes) than the other two, so the initial presentation of selected scenes from *Black Narcissus* communicates a more comprehensive account of the characters, their dilemmas and temptations. It is perhaps unexpected that an avant-garde film should be interested in the linear progression of the narrative of *Black Narcissus*. But as we have seen, this serves as a parallel narrative for the developing relationship between the nun and artist of *Damned if You Don't*. The combination of the down-graded images from *Black Narcissus* and the voiceover summary of the plot serve to 'present' the film in one of its 'versions', how it would have been seen when first broadcast on television. This implies a different viewing experience from the other two films that emphasise *Black Narcissus* as an intensely *cinematic* event. Since the artist is watching the film at the start of *Damned if You Don't* at the beginning of her own personal journey, it is appropriate that the mode of viewing *Black Narcissus* is a private one, reminding us of the powerful and fondly remembered impressions often made by old films when watched on television. All three appropriations share the same sense of a film that is strikingly memorable, whether first seen on television in black-and-white, in a cinema on first release or in its fully restored, pristine-like form.

Black Narcissus has therefore had many incarnations, whether at the hands of the censors or through conscious reworkings of some of its most compelling scenes. It continues to be remarkable, as an indicator of state-of-the-art special effects, designs and use of Technicolor in the 1940s, as an evocative end-of-empire film, a popular melodrama and source for experimental film-making. It survived Rumer Godden's disapproval, censors' cuts and critics' ambivalence. As part of the general revival of interest in Powell and Pressburger's work it benefited from the critical turn to *auteur* analysis. In more recent years it has arguably gained an even higher status for an enhanced appreciation of the work of their collaborators, particularly Alfred Junge, Hein Heckroth, Jack Cardiff and the actors. Michael Powell called it 'an almost perfect film', explaining that 'there is always something lost in even the finest film, or perhaps I should write, especially in the finest film'.[17] While he is referring to the deletion of the scene between Sister Clodagh and Mother Superior that would have been placed at the end of the film (see Chapter Two, pp. 59–60), the sentiment can be extended to the film more generally in a positive way. Perhaps the best films are *never* those that are 'complete' or self-contained, but instead lend themselves to re-evaluation, to what can be gained through research, appropriation and reinvention. Godden felt that the novel had a similarly poignant resonance in connection with her own creativity: 'I knew that this happy and exhilarating time of *Black Narcissus* could not last – of all that it had meant to me in ecstasy, excitement and growth it is impossible to tell.'[18] Indeed, it is this unfinished sensibility of *Black Narcissus* that lingers, particularly as I have argued in the film's ambivalent closure, its unsettling atmosphere, blurring of boundaries between characters, scenes and settings. This representational mode explains its enduring appeal and significance in the canon of Powell and Pressburger's films and in British cinema.

FIVE
Conclusion

Black Narcissus is characterised by unstable boundaries that question many apparent certainties and notions of 'truth'. A terrifying precipice is in fact only a few feet above the ground; a bell that purports to keep time cannot function as such when it is drowned out by competing sounds, and flowers filmed in Surrey masquerade as Indian blooms – the Eastern 'Other' is in fact an English garden. Characters in the film also are not what they seem. Mopu has a profound effect on Clodagh, Ruth and the other nuns, revealing their vulnerabilities and leading them to question their mission. They believe that the local people desire a Western education and medical treatment, but we discover that the General has paid them to attend. In this and other respects *Black Narcissus* is remarkable as an 'end of empire' film, conveying the fissures and contradictions of that complex historical process, which had not been so clearly delineated in previous films with colonial settings.[1]

Serving as a powerful indicator of the contemporary Western imagination's idea of India, Junge's designs excelled in their artifice. Yet everything being so 'exaggerated' opens up place and space to a variety of meanings. The carefully constructed environment as a seductive, remarkable place that Western influence cannot tame or repress is a key element of the film's ambiguous address. At times Mopu is beautiful, uncannily familiar to the West, while on other occasions we see it as threatening, exemplified by the incessant wind and causing the nuns to suffer from strange illnesses. The place therefore serves almost as a character with its momentous impact on the nuns. In contrast to their brief stay we are reminded of Mopu's permanence, with its predictable rhythms of sunshine, rain and snow that appear to determine the length of their stay (Mr Dean: 'I'll give you until the rains break') and the extent of their involvement with the local people. When Tony Williams asked Michael Powell whether the nuns were in part destroyed by the nature of the environment he acknowledged that 'It was because of the *special* environment. They were obviously successful down in Calcutta … But when they were put in this extraordinary windy palace it was too much for them – the atmosphere and the loneliness and, as they say, the wind.'[2] As we have seen, this particular construction of place marks the film as distinctive. In their desire to compensate for not shooting on location, the technical team excelled at creating a persuasive, yet artificial world. This led to somewhat contradictory acknowledgements in publicity material. While the pressbook declared that 'Messrs. Powell and Pressburger have taken full advantage of the locale' without actually admitting that they had not filmed in India, Herb Lightman, writing in *American Cinematographer*, revealed: 'One of the most outstanding photographic features of *Black Narcissus* is the camera treatment of the majestic Himalayan scenery. These scenes become almost incredible when one considers that they were all filmed *in England* by means of *backdrops*.'[3] Indeed, it is this collapsing of the 'real' and artifice, and the centrality of place in the film's narrative that makes the depiction of India so remarkable in *Black Narcissus*.

Other formal devices work towards making the film a complex meditation on the British withdrawal from India. Whereas on first examination the film might appear to be constructing an entirely Orientalist conception of the East as 'Other', I have argued that the flashbacks in particular work to complicate this binary in intriguing ways. Crucially, the flashbacks all have a connection with the present, containing affective moments that collapse time and space. As we have seen, the hunt scene has a sound overlap that announces the arrival of the young General and, as Williams has noted, Clodagh's 'narcissistic look' into the mirror when she has put on the jewellery given to her by her grandmother in Ireland 'evokes Kanchi's flirtatious gazes at herself in the mirror when she sees the young General' who we know reminds Clodagh of Con.[4] Even the frame becoming totally black as she runs out to meet Con can be linked to a later usage of the same technique when Ruth collapses in Mr Dean's house. In this way a complex East–West connection is established, unusual in films set in colonial contexts. In colonialist discourse depictions of 'the East' are far more troubling when not firmly separated from Western experience. As we have seen, this causes Sister Clodagh extreme anxiety when she begins to connect past and present, West and East. Without the flashbacks the film becomes far more conventional, since they reveal an uncomfortable acknowledgement that one of the key ideological underpinnings of colonialism is breaking down, that it is no longer tenable.

Also contributing to the film's questioning of Western attitudes is the depiction of 'natives', which does not consist entirely of stereotypes. While there is no doubt that many of these characters do fall into this category in their childlike demeanour, their non-speaking roles and peripheral placement in the narrative, there are also levels of complexity associated with some of them that take the film beyond the norm in this respect. The values associated with organised religion are severely questioned by the example of the Holy Man, even though Sister Clodagh's faith is not destroyed.

As discussed in Chapter Two, Kanchi's sexuality can be read as conforming to a stereotype of rapacious native sexual appetites, but when contrasted with Sister Ruth's desires – depicted as mad, associated with illness, sadness and violence – they acquire a natural, unrepressed and celebratory status. This is rewarded when she succeeds in claiming the young General, their love affair being a key aspect of his decision to live like his ancestors. In this he acquires dignity, since he breaks with his former characterisation as a simple Anglophile whose cultural misunderstandings provide humour (his desire to be taught physics by 'the physical Sister'; congratulating Sister Clodagh on the birth of Christ).

Black Narcissus can therefore be read as an extremely 'open' text, which explains its suitability for appropriation. As Chapter Four demonstrates, it provides a rich source of images, sensibilities and associations that can be transformed into new meanings. The dominant theme to be drawn upon in this way is the sexual repression dynamic associated with Sister Ruth, rather than the colonial context. The force of the scenes between Deborah Kerr and Kathleen Byron tend to dominate the film's reputation as a melodrama about sexual repression in the Himalayas. Yet in the three examples discussed in Chapter Four, Ruth can be seen to triumph. In *Damned if You Don't* the parallel narrative of the nun and artist ends in a sexual union that was denied to her in *Black Narcissus*; in *A Bit of Scarlet* the literal placement of Clodagh and Ruth in an overt context of lesbian desire shifts the 'transformation' scene to another level of intensity that is celebratory rather than pathological, and in *Remembering Sister Ruth* Kathleen Byron's defence of her character, and her desire to be seen as largely responsible for the creation of her screen persona, contribute to the memory of Ruth as the most compelling character in the film. In a way she has defied her screen death in *Black Narcissus* by being resuscitated in Venville's film.

Yet working against these 'open' elements that locate *Black Narcissus* as a film that very much questions assumptions about the primacy of the West, the right of Westerners to exercise control in the East and the finality of the film's narrative closure, is the question of Mr Dean. As argued in Chapter Two, his authority is a significant factor in countering the power of the 'hysterical' forces unleashed by the place and its impact on the nuns. He represents a particular type of British involvement in India, and this is undisturbed by the establishment of St Faith at Mopu. He remains there as they leave and he dominates the final shots of the film. It is possible to interpret this authoritative narrative role as offsetting the range of complexities outlined above. His form of British presence in India is vindicated, even though it has connections with colonialism and colonial attitudes. His masculinity is coded as 'real' in comparison with the feminisation, and therefore weakening, of the young General. As his embarrassing, colluding accomplice, Angu Ayah, confirms in a film all about uncertainty, misreading people and situations, Mr Dean was right. When reading the film as an unstable colonial text it is important therefore to acknowledge the effect of Mr Dean and what he represents. But as I have argued in Chapter Two, it is also extremely significant that in comparison with the novel the film's closure is more 'open', since it excludes scenes that emphasise the renewal of Clodagh's spirit and resolve to do missionary work elsewhere in India. As such the film operates as a site of hybridity, demonstrating the processes of 'resignification' identified by Bagchi in relation to the novel, but to an even greater extent. The young General, for example, tries to be 'English' and aspires to Western norms, but these are revealed to be flawed, even ridiculous, as the education being offered by the nuns is clearly inappropriate. Drawing on the post-colonial theories of Homi Bhabha, *Black Narcissus* offers an apposite case-study of the ways in which the 'civilising mission' is irrecoverably disrupted by unforeseen factors, resulting in a displacement of authority and a general calling into question of the entire enterprise.[5] When compared with British films of the 1950s that sought to equate empire with the introduction of liberal values and modernisation while emphasising productive British–Indian collaboration, *Black Narcissus* is far less assured in its message.[6]

As a Powell and Pressburger film *Black Narcissus* also raises interesting questions about boundaries in relation to its own production history. This reveals the full extent of collaboration, particularly once the decision to film in Horsham and Pinewood had been taken. While Powell gave fair recognition to the work of collaborators in his autobiography, studying the film's genesis, planning, shooting and release suggests an even greater sense of collective creative responsibility. In an analysis that has privileged the role of place as especially significant, Jack Cardiff, Hein Heckroth and Alfred Junge emerge as key experts who ably demonstrated their skills in overcoming many obstacles to achieve the desired effect. Cardiff and Junge were rewarded in the form of three Academy Awards (cinematography, art and set direction). Herb Lightman even went so far as to declare it as 'definitely *a cameraman's picture*'.[7] And, before production commenced, Rumer Godden's novel provided the source text that remained relatively unchanged – with a few notable exceptions – in its adaptation for the screen. Whether viewed from an auteurist perspective, as a key British melodrama of the 1940s or as a film with political resonance in relation to decolonisation, *Black Narcissus* remains as controversial and fascinating as it was on first release in 1947.

Notes

1. ORIGINS

1. Godden, *A Time to Dance, No Time to Weep*, pp. 129-30.

2. Godden, *Black Narcissus*, p. 19.

3. Ibid., p. 9.

4. Ibid., p. 26.

5. Ibid., p. 46.

6. Ibid., p. 123.

7. Ibid., p. 78.

8. Ibid., p. 69.

9. Ibid., p. 204.

10. Chisholm, *Rumer Godden*, pp. 91–2.

11. Godden, *A Time to Dance, No Time to Weep*, p. 132.

12. Ibid., pp. 81–93 and Chrisholm, *Rumer Godden*, p. 63.

13. Ibid., p. 92.

14. Said, *Orientalism*, p. 244.

15. See Richards, '"Patriotism with Profit"', pp. 245–56.

16. Chowdhry, *Colonial India and the Making of Empire Cinema*, p. 2.

17. Landy, *British Genres*, p. 97.

18. Street, *British National Cinema*, p. 46.

19. Shohat and Stam, *Unthinking Eurocentrism*, p. 166.

20. Chowdhry, *Colonial India and the Making of Empire Cinema*, p. 8.

21. Dyer, *White*, p. 184.

22. Kevin Gough-Yates, for example, describes *Black Narcissus* as 'an almost arche-typal Powell/Pressburger film. The nuns deceive themselves about the nature of the world yet it forces its way through to their consciousness. From the convent in the Palace of Mopu, the Sisters see more clearly than they have been doing, the way their emotions, their sexuality, concepts of beauty, all of which are in this world, conflict with their pride. In this way the overall idea is connected with their earlier films.' National Film Theatre programme notes, BFI Library.

23. For an excellent study of this film see Cook, *I Know Where I'm Going!*

24. Powell, *A Life in Movies*, p. 558.

25. Ibid., p. 559.

26. Macdonald, *Emeric Pressburger*, p. 265.

27. Chisholm, *Rumer Godden*, p. 194. It is interesting that Godden foresaw difficulties with censorship.

28. *Variety*, 23 September 1942.

29. Godden, *A House with Four Rooms*, p. 52.

30. Chisholm, *Rumer Godden*, p. 201.

31. Godden, *A House with Four Rooms*, p. 63. This figure is a little lower than the one quoted in the Michael Powell Special Collection, BFI Library documents, box 4, item S-71: Budget. In this document the figure given for story rights is £2,020.

32. See Macnab, *J. Arthur Rank*, pp. 122-31.

33. Powell, *A Life in Movies*, pp. 562-3.

34. Ibid., p. 562.

35. Macdonald, *Emeric Pressburger*, p. 266.

36. Powell, *A Life in Movies*, pp. 159, 584 and Chrisholm, *Rumer Godden*, p. 201.

37. Interview with Jack Cardiff in 'Painting with Light', documentary directed by Craig McCall (Modus Operandi Films and Smoke & Mirrors Film Productions, 2000), reproduced on Criterion DVD of *Black Narcissus*. Cardiff also recounted this incident to Justin Bowyer in *Conversations with Jack Cardiff*, pp. 40–1.

38. Petrie, 'Neo-expressionism and British Cinematography: The Work of Robert Krasker and Jack Cardiff', in Orr and Taxidou (eds), *Post War Cinema and Modernity*, p. 230 and Petrie, *The British Cinematographer*, p. 40.

39. Interview with Scorsese in McCall's 'Painting with Light' documentary, 2000.

40. Godden, *A House with Four Rooms*, p. 52.

41. See Petrie, *The British Cinematographer*, pp. 80–2.

42. Bergfelder in Cook, *Gainsborough Studios*, p. 33.

43. For a discussion of Junge's designs for *A Matter of Life and Death* see Christie, *A Matter of Life and Death*, pp. 43–9.

44. Powell, *A Life in Movies*, p. 544. Junge was assisted by Ivor Beddoes, a sketch artist who also worked on *Black Narcissus*. Some of the set drawings held at the National Film Archive, Berkhamstead, are signed by Beddoes.

45. Powell, *A Life in Movies*, p. 628.

46. Michael Powell Special Collection, box 4, item S-71: Budget. British Film Institute Library.

47. Powell, *A Life in Movies*, p. 545.

48. Pressbook, *Black Narcissus*, British Film Institute Library.

49. Ibid.

50. Godden, *A House with Four Rooms*, pp. 52-3. In spite of these comments it is interesting, however, to note that in *Black Narcissus* Godden describes the young General as wearing 'fabulous' coats and jewels, p. 123.

51. Lightman, '*Black Narcissus*: Color Masterpiece', p. 457.

52. See the Hein Heckroth designs for *Black Narcissus* located at the National Film Archive, Berkamsted, London.

53. Powell, *A Life in Movies*, p. 311.

54. Cardiff interviewed by Bowyer, *Conversations with Jack Cardiff*, p. 73.

55. Macdonald, *Emeric Pressburger*, p. 269.

56. Powell, *A Life in Movies*, pp. 581–2.

57. Ibid., p. 581.

58. Ibid., p. 583

59. Cardiff interviewed by Bowyer, *Conversations with Jack Cardiff*, p. 80.

60. Byron, interviewed by McFarlane, *An Autobiography of British Cinema*, p. 105.

61. According to Kathleen Byron the part had first been offered to Pamela Brown. After Byron had read the script Powell offered it to her instead. See *Remembering Sister Ruth*, a film by Malcolm Venville, Popular Films, 1997, broadcast on BBC2 and discussed in Chapter Four.

62. Macdonald, *Emeric Pressburger*, p. 267. This divergence of opinion is also mentioned in *Remembering Sister Ruth*. See discussion in Chapter Four.

63. BFI Special Collection, Michael Powell, box 4, A-S-68, 'corrections to script in Emeric Pressburger's handwriting', n.d.

64. Powell, *A Life in Movies*, pp. 413, 512.

65. Ibid., p. 574.

66. Michael Powell Special Collection, box 4, item S-71: Budget. British Film Institute Library.

67. Powell, *A Life in Movies*, p. 579. The reference to Livesey is indicated in Pressburger's 'corrections' to the script, BFI Special Collection, box 4, A-S-68, n.d. The reference to Donat is in a telegram from Pressburger to Powell, 4 January 1946: 'Donat reading *Narcissus*. Want to know how strongly you feel on this subject.' BFI Special Collection, Pressburger, item 23(g).

68. Farrar interviewed by McFarlane, *An Autobiography of British Cinema*, p. 184.

69. See 'Corrections to Screenplay by Emeric Pressburger', BFI Special Collection, Michael Powell, box 4, A-S-68, n.d.

70. Chowdhry, *Colonial India*, p. 89.

71. Ibid., p. 91.

72. For a full account of the reception of *The Drum* in India see ibid., pp. 57–123.

73. Powell, *A Life in Movies*, p. 580.

74. For details of Sabu's career see article by Liebfred in *Films in Review*, pp. 451–7.

For the resentment of his roles in India see Chowdhry, *Colonial India*, pp. 89–91.

75. Godden, *A House with Four Rooms*, p. 52.

76. See Shohat and Stam, *Unthinking Eurocentrism*, pp. 139-40.

77. Pressbook, *Black Narcissus*, British Film Institute Library.

78. Eddie Whaley Jr was born in the UK. He was the son of Eddie Whaley, an actor who appeared in *Kentucky Minstrels* (1934) with Harry Scott. Whaley and Scott came to the UK in 1909 and went on to become a popular BBC radio double act.

79. Powell, *A Life in Movies*, p. 581.

80. Pressbook, *Black Narcissus*, British Film Institute Library.

81. Powell, *A Life in Movies*, p. 574.

82. Godden, *A House with Four Rooms*, p. 52.

83. Michael Powell Special Collection, box 4, item S-72. British Film Institute Library.

84. Powell, *A Life in Movies*, p. 563.

85. Pressbook, *Black Narcissus*, British Film Institute Library.

86. Lightman, '*Black Narcissus*: Color Masterpiece', p. 433.

87. Ibid., p. 456.

88. Godden, *Black Narcissus*, p. 21.

89. For Godden's reaction to Junge's designs see Godden, *A House with Four Rooms*, pp. 51–3.

90. For a discussion of the development of Technicolor see Christie, *A Matter of Life and Death*, pp. 41–2.

91. Cardiff interviewed by Bowyer, *Conversations with Jack Cardiff*, p. 74.

92. Interview with Cardiff in McCall's 'Painting with Light' documentary, 2000.

93. The editor was Reginald Mills who had worked with Powell and Pressburger on *A Matter of Life and Death*. He went on to work with them on several subsequent films, including *The Red Shoes*, *The Tales of Hoffmann* and *Oh Rosalinda!!*.

94. Tony Williams asked Michael Powell whether *Black Narcissus* was 'a critique of British insularity and imperialism along with the sexual repression themes'. He replied, 'Not really. There was none of that in the book and we admired the book very much … It was very well balanced about the Indians and the British.' *Films and Filming*, 1981, p. 13.

95. Godden, *Black Narcissus*, p. 224.

2. ANALYSIS

1. For a consideration of the film in relation to other imperial films see Jaikumar, '"Place" and the Modernist Redemption of Empire', pp. 57–77, a key article

on *Black Narcissus* that also emphasises the importance of place as an unsettling aspect of the film.

2. Bhabha, *The Location of Culture*. For a discussion of Bhabha's main ideas see Kraniauskas, 'Hybridity in a Transnational Frame', pp. 235–56.

3. Godden, *Black Narcissus*, p. 57.

4. A typical painting by Vermeer that uses this technique is 'Woman Holding a Balance', *c*. 1664.

5. Godden, *Black Narcissus*, p. 11.

6. Jaikumar, '"Place" and the Modernist Redemption of Empire', p. 60.

7. Jaikumar, Ibid., p. 59.

8. Godden, *Black Narcissus*, p. 21.

9. Ibid., p. 11.

10. At one point during script development Pressburger wanted the bell being drowned out by horns to appear again towards the end of the film. BFI Special Collection, Michael Powell, box 4, A-S-68, 'corrections to script in Emeric Pressburger's handwriting', n.d.

11. Bhabha, *The Location of Culture*, p. 105.

12. Bagchi, 'Of Nuns and Palaces', pp. 55–6.

13. For associations between non-white women and libidinous desire see Shohat and Stam, *Unthinking Eurocentrism*, pp. 156–7, 169.

14. Kraniauskas, 'Hybridity in a Transnational Frame', p. 241.

15. Godden, *Black Narcissus*, p. 81.

16. Street, *Transatlantic Crossings*, pp. 129-31.

17. Durgnat, '*Black Narcissus*: Retrospective', p. 313

18. Turim, *Flashbacks in Film*, p. 15.

19. The construction of this scene was not always like this. In his 'corrections' to the script Pressburger had Sister Clodagh in her office writing to Mother Dorothea and then 'Sister Philippa staring at mountain with spade, she begins to work. Clodagh goes down to garden. Philippa's hands.' BFI Special Collection, Michael Powell, box 4, A-S-68, n.d.

20. It was a recurrent trope in melodramas of the 1940s that a female character would 'lose herself' when playing the piano, even indicating a split personality/ *alter ego*, as, for example in *A Place of One's Own* (1945, starring Margaret Lockwood).

21. Godden, *Black Narcissus*, p. 90.

22. The Society of Army and Navy Stores was founded in 1871 to provide basic and luxury items for British servicemen and their families. Branches were opened in the colonies, including India (Bombay, Calcutta, Simla and Madras had branches). In the 1930s members of the public like the young General were able to purchase items from the stores. His acquisition of the perfume is indicative of his Anglophile sympathies, as well as serving as an allusion to the 'informal' imperialism represented by such a commercial institution.

23. Walker, '*Black Narcissus*', p. 10.

24. The censors in Pennsylvania deleted these lines, however. PCA file, Herrick, local censor board reports.

25. See Turim, *Flashbacks in Film*.

26. Jaikumar, '"Place" and the Modernist Redemption of Empire', p. 66.

27. Walker, '*Black Narcissus*', pp. 11–12.

28. Macdonald, *Emeric Pressburger*, p. 267.

29. This association with horror is also highlighted by Walker, '*Black Narcissus*', p. 10.

30. This strategy is repeated in the scene in which Clodagh watches over Ruth when she has changed into her ordinary clothes and is putting on lipstick. Again, the Bible acts as a symbol between them.

31. Byron interviewed by McFarlane, 1990 in *An Autobiography of British Cinema*, p. 105.

32. On the Criterion DVD copy of *Black Narcissus* Martin Scorsese comments that this strategy of characters appearing to 'jump into the frame' influenced him when shooting *The Color of Money* (1986).

33. The boots were a present to them all from Mr Dean. This detail is in the book and included by Pressburger in his 'corrections' to the script, but the gesture never reached the final film. BFI Special Collection, Powell, box 4, A-S-68, n.d.

34. It was Kathleen Byron's idea to have Ruth walk about Mr Dean's place and pick up some of his things. See *Remembering Sister Ruth*, discussed in Chapter Four.

35. Petrie in Orr and Taxidou, *Post War Cinema and Modernity*, p. 231.

36. The novel makes more of Ruth's horrible death as Godden describes her falling on a bamboo spike, driven through her chest. See Godden, *Black Narcissus*, p. 205.

37. Shohat and Stam, *Unthinking Eurocentrism*, p. 166.

38. When Mr Dean comments on the Holy Man in the novel he speaks of God creating the stream and that Christ would not remove him from his post, even though it is on land occupied by the convent (pp. 60–3). Pantheism is directly referred to when Sister Adela describes the young General's religious beliefs as 'a form of pantheism' (p. 152).

39. Godden, *Black Narcissus*, p. 85.

40. Ibid., p. 15.

41. Bagchi, 'Of Nuns and Palaces', pp. 57, 64.

42. See Jaikumar, '"Place" and the Modernist Redemption of Empire' and Shohat and Stam, *Unthinking Eurocentrism*, p. 166.

43. When Mr Dean delivers Kanchi to the convent there is an implication that she has offered herself to him sexually. Whether he has taken this up is left ambiguous but a source of gentle amusement. Mr Dean asks Clodagh, 'Are

you sure there's no question you've been dying to ask me?', to which she resolutely replies, 'None!'

44. Powell, *A Life in Movies*, pp. 623–64. This scene is referred to as an 'epilogue' by Pressburger in his early corrections to the script, see BFI Special Collection, Michael Powell, box 4, A-S-68, n.d.

45. Godden, *Black Narcissus*, pp. 207–8.

46. Interview with Cardiff in McCall's 'Painting with Light' documentary, 2000. See also Petrie, *The British Cinematographer*, p. 77.

47. Powell, *A Life in Movies*, p. 624.

48. Godden, *Black Narcissus*, p. 207.

49. Ibid., p. 210.

50. Bagchi, 'Of Nuns and Palaces'.

51. Durgnat, '*Black Narcissus*: Retrospective', p. 313.

3. RECEPTION

1. *Daily Telegraph* review, quoted in Macdonald, *Emeric Pressburger*, p. 272.

2. *Sight and Sound*, 16 (61), Spring 1947, p. 76.

3. C. A. Lejeune, quoted in Macdonald, *Emeric Pressburger*, pp. 271–2.

4. *Kinematograph Weekly*, 24 April 1947, p. 27 and *The Cinema*, 23 April 1947, pp. 3, 36.

5. Macdonald, *Emeric Pressburger*, p. 271. See also R. H. 'Josh' Billings' annual survey in *Kinematograph Weekly*, which listed *Black Narcissus* as one of the year's 'outstanding releases', 'a notable box-office attraction' with Deborah Kerr and David Farrar included in the 'most popular and consistent star' list, 8 December 1947, pp. 13–14. Similarly, Thumim's box-office survey, based on a variety of trade paper polls, lists *Black Narcissus* as one of 1947's most popular films in Britain. See *Screen*, 1991, p. 258.

6. Street, *Transatlantic Crossings*, pp. 97–8.

7. Robert Boothby, *Parliamentary Debates* (Commons), vol. 415, col. 2539, 6 November 1945.

8. For details of the Dalton Duty Crisis see Street, *British National Cinema*, pp.14–15 and Dickinson and Street, *Cinema and State*, pp. 186–95.

9. A shorter account of the American censorship of *Black Narcissus* was first published in Street, *Transatlantic Crossings*, pp. 124–31.

10. See Maltby in Nowell-Smith (ed.), *The Oxford History of World Cinema*, pp. 235–48).

11. Black, *The Catholic Crusade Against the Movies*, p. 5.

12. For details of *The Outlaw* case see ibid., pp. 37–43.

13. 20 April 1945, PCA file on *Black Narcissus*, Margaret Herrick Library, Los Angeles.

14. 26 April 1945, ibid.

15. Ibid.

16. Breen to Allen (Rank Organisation), 17 April 1946, ibid.

17. Powell and Pressburger to Breen, 25 May 1946, ibid.

18. 5 June 1947, ibid.

19. Breen to Pressburger, 1 October 1946, report of advice given to McLafferty, ibid.

20. I am grateful to John Hill for providing me with this reference.

21. 10 April 1946, LOD file on *Black Narcissus*, Margaret Herrick Library, Los Angeles.

22. 10 April and 19 July 1946, ibid.

23. 8 July 1947, ibid.

24. 11 July 1947, ibid.

25. 23 July 1947, ibid.

26. 20 July 1947, LOD and PCA.

27. Eleanor Lewis to Miss Taylore (Breen's secretary), n.d., PCA.

28. See memos dated 20 June and 19 July 1947, Universal archive, University of Southern California, box 411/17/12704.

29. Mrs Bradberry, Assistant to the Chairlady of the Motion Picture Council of Protestant Women, informed the Johnston office (MPAA) that *Black Narcissus* was 'a wonderful film'. See memo from Masterson to Cardinal Spellman, 8 August 1947, LOD.

30. Lloyd L. Sloan reporting in the *Citizen News*, 8 July 1947.

31. See *Los Angeles Herald*, 8 July 1947.

32. 5 August 1947, LOD. A press release to this effect was issued, 14 August 1947.

33. 6 August 1947, LOD. Report by John O'Connor.

34. *LA Times*, 12 August 1947.

35. 26 September 1947, LOD.

36. See memo from Masterson to Cardinal Spellman, 8 August 1947, ibid.

37. See Masterson to Rev. Hugh A. Donohoe, Diocesan Director, LOD, San Francisco, 19 September 1947, ibid.

38. See reactions to the ban, ibid.

39. See memo by Masterson, 26 September 1947, ibid.

40. *Variety* reported on 5 November 1947 that Pressburger visited New York and had talks with representatives of the LOD. He is said to have brought with him an Italian version of the film that had been approved by the Vatican. I have not been able to trace a copy.

41. Although the PCA file reveals that the local censor board in Pennsylvania deleted some of the dialogue from this scene, Sister Clodagh's comment: 'But

in a little place like that – and I had shown him I loved him – I had to get away first'.

42. Herbert Morris in the *New York Times*, 21 March 1948, p. 5.

43. Editor's comment on Morris's letter, The *New York Times*, 21 Mar 1948, p. 5. The Powell telegram, 18 November 1947, states: 'Censor has okayed new version *Narcissus*. Please clarify which version will be acceptable in Latin America. Hope not USA version', in Pressburger Special Collection, BFI, box 6, item 10 (G).

44. William K. Everson, programme notes for *Black Narcissus*, 1980, Museum of Modern Art, New York.

45. *Variety*, 9 August 1947 and *American Cinematographer*, December 1947.

46. *New York Times*, 17 August 1947.

47. *New Movies*, National Board of Review, XXII (5) October 1947, pp. 6–7.

48. *New York Herald Tribune*, 14 August 1947.

49. *Time*, 25 August 1947.

50. *New York Times*, 14 August 1947 and *Time*, 25 August 1947.

51. Macdonald, *Emeric Pressburger*, p. 292.

52. Said, *Orientalism*, p. 4.

4. REVIVAL AND APPROPRIATION

1. See Petley, 'The Lost Continent', in Barr (ed.), *All Our Yesterdays*, p. 106. In the DVD commentary on *Black Narcissus* Scorsese talks about the thrill he experienced when he saw a restored colour print, rendering the flashback sequence in Ireland particularly vivid.

2. Christie, writing in the Foreword to Powell, *Million-Dollar Movie*, p. viii.

3. *Damned if You Don't* was produced by grants from the New York State Council on the Arts, the Jerome Foundation and the German Academic Exchange Service. It appeared in many international film festivals and won prizes for Best Experimental Film at the 1990 Athens Film Festival and at the 1998 Atlanta Film Festival. It is Friedrich's fourth 16mm film. Her previous films were *Cool Hands, Warm Heart* (1979), *Gently Down the Stream* (1981) and *The Ties That Bind* (1984).

4. *Afterimage*, May 1988, p. 9.

5. Ibid.

6. This connection is made by Scott Macdonald in the *Afterimage* interview. P. Adams Sitney wrote an influential book on avant-garde film entitled *Visionary Film: The American Avant-Garde*, 2nd edn 1979.

7. *Afterimage* interview, p. 8.

8. See Street, *British National Cinema*, p. 175.

9. Script of *Damned if You Don't*, <http://www.sufriedrich.com>.

10. Ibid.

11. The Legion of Decency had ceased to exist by 1975.

12. Andrea Weiss, correspondence with author, 12 August 2003.

13. The quotation is from Powell, *Million-Dollar Movie*, p. 16.

14. In this film she confirms, however, that her relationship with Powell was sexual, even though he implies in his autobiography that it was not.

15. Byron interviewed by Brian McFarlane in *Autobiography of British Cinema*, p. 105.

16. Godden, *A Time to Dance, No Time to Weep*, p. 132.

17. Powell, *A Life in Movies*, p. 623.

18. Godden, *A Time to Dance, No Time to Weep*, p. 138.

5. CONCLUSION

1. Jaikumar, ' "Place" and the Modernist Redemption of Empire' also makes this key point.

2. Powell quoted in Williams, *Structures of Desire*, p. 124.

3. *Black Narcissus* pressbook and Lightman, '*Black Narcissus*: Colour Masterpiece', *American Cinematographer*, p. 433.

4. Williams, *Structures of Desire*, p. 132.

5. Bagchi, 'Of Nuns and Palaces', pp. 53–5 and Bhabha, *The Location of Culture*, p. 114.

6. For a discussion of British films with imperial themes made in the 1950s see Chowdhry, *Colonial India*, pp. 251–55.

7. Lightman, '*Black Narcissus*: Colour Masterpiece', p. 432.

Sources

PRIMARY SOURCES

Michael Powell Special Collection: British Film Institute Library, London

Emeric Pressburger Special Collection: British Film Institute Library, London

Alfred Junge and Hein Heckroth designs: National Film Archive, Berkhamstead

Alfred Junge designs: The Bibliothèque du Film (Bifi), Paris

Production Code Administration and Legion of Decency files: The Margaret Herrick Library, Motion Picture Academy Foundation, Los Angeles

The Museum of Modern Art, New York

Universal Studios Archive: University of Southern California, Los Angeles

BOOKS AND ARTICLES

Bagchi, 'Of Nuns and Palaces: Rumer Godden's *Black Narcissus*', *Christianity and Literature*, 45 (1), Autumn 1995

Bergfelder, Tim, 'Surface and Distraction: Style and Genre in Gainsborough in the Late 1920s and 1930s', in Pam Cook (ed.), *Gainsborough Pictures* (London, 1997)

Bhabha, Homi, *The Location of Culture* (London, 1994)

Black, Gregory, *The Catholic Crusade Against the Movies, 1940–75* (Cambridge, 1997)

Bowyer, Justin, *Conversations with Jack Cardiff: Art, Light and Direction in Cinema* (London, 2003)

Brown, Judith C., *Immodest Acts: The Life of a Lesbian Nun in Renaissance Italy* (New York, 1986)

Chisholm, Anne, *Rumer Godden: A Storyteller's Life* (London, 1998)

Chowdhry, Prem, *Colonial India and the Making of Empire Cinema: Image, Ideology, Identity* (Manchester, 2000)

Christie, Ian, *A Matter of Life and Death* (London, 2000)

Cook, Pam, *I Know Where I'm Going!* (London, 2002)

Dickinson, Margaret and Sarah Street, *Cinema and State: The Film Industry and the British Government, 1927–84* (London, 1985)

Durgnat, Raymond, '*Black Narcissus*: Retrospective', *Monthly Film Bulletin*, 51 (609), 1984

Dyer, Richard, *White* (London, 1997)

Godden, Rumer, *Black Narcissus* (London, 1939; 1994 Pan Books edition)

Godden, Rumer, *A Time to Dance, No Time to Weep* (London, 1987)

— *A House with Four Rooms* (London, 1989)

Jaikumar, Priya, '"Place" and the Modernist Redemption of Empire in *Black Narcissus*', *Cinema Journal*, 40 (2), Winter 2001

Kraniauskas, John, ' Hybridity in a Transnational Frame: Latin-Americanist and Post-colonial Perspectives on Cultural Studies' in A. Brah and A. Coombes (eds), *Hybridity and Its Discontents: Politics, Science, Culture* (London and New York, 2000)

Landy, Marcia, *British Genres: Cinema and Society, 1930–1960* (Princeton, New Jersey, 1991)

Liebfred, Philip, 'Sabu', *Films in Review*, 40 (10), October 1989

Lightman, Herb, '*Black Narcissus*: Color Masterpiece', *American Cinematographer*, December 1947

Macdonald, Kevin, *Emeric Pressburger: The Life and Death of a Screenwriter* (London, 1994)

McFarlane, Brian, *An Autobiography of British Cinema* (London, 1997)

Macnab, Geoffrey, *J. Arthur Rank and the British Film Industry* (London, 1993)

Maltby, Richard, 'Censorship and Self-regulation', in Geoffrey Nowell-Smith (ed.), *The Oxford History of World Cinema* (Oxford, 1996)

Petley, Julian, 'The Lost Continent', in Charles Barr (ed.), *All Our Yesterdays: 90 Years of British Cinema* (London, 1998)

Petrie, Duncan, *The British Cinematographer* (London, 1996)

— 'Neo-expressionism and British Cinematography: The Work of Robert Krasker and Jack Cardiff', in John Orr and Olga Taxidou (eds), *Post War Cinema and Modernity* (Exeter, 2000)

Powell, Michael, *A Life in Movies* (London, 1986)

— *Million-Dollar Movie* (London, 1992)

Richards, Jeffrey, '"Patriotism with Profit": British Imperial Cinema in the 1930s', in James Curran and Vincent Porter (eds), *British Cinema History* (London, 1983)

Said, Edward W., *Orientalism: Western Conceptions of the Orient* (London, 1995 edn)

Shohat, Ella and Robert Stam *Unthinking Eurocentrism: Multiculturalism and the Media* (London, 1994)

Street, Sarah, *British National Cinema* (London, 1997)

— *Transatlantic Crossings: British Feature Films in the USA* (New York and London, 2002)

Thumim, Janet, 'The "Popular", Cash and Culture in the Post-war British Cinema Industry', *Screen*, 32 (3), Autumn 1991

Turim, Maureen, *Flashbacks in Film: Memory and History* (London, 1989)

Walker, Michael, '*Black Narcissus*', *Framework*, 9, Winter 1978–79

Williams, Tony, interview with Michael Powell, *Films and Filming*, 326, November 1981

— *Structures of Desire: British Cinema, 1939–55* (Albany, 2000)